War and Civilization

SELECTED BY ALBERT V. FOWLER

A STUDY OF HISTORY *and this selection from it*
are issued under the auspices
of the Royal Institute of International Affairs.
The Royal Institute of International Affairs
is an unofficial and non-political body,
founded in 1920 to encourage and facilitate
the scientific study of international questions.
The Institute, as such, is precluded by its rules
from expressing an opinion on any aspect
of international affairs;
opinions expressed in this book are, therefore,
purely individual.

ARNOLD J. TOYNBEE

War and Civilization

———

FROM A STUDY OF HISTORY

NEW YORK

Oxford University Press

1950

Only here and there throughout the course of the six volumes of *A Study of History* does Mr. Toynbee assume the role of prophet, pointing out to his fellows the grave consequences of their acts and calling them to repent of their waywardness. When some of these scattered passages are culled out and fitted together and brought to bear on the single problem of War in our contemporary life, Mr. Toynbee stands forth in the full power and eloquence of his prophetic role. Here he is examining in the long perspective of the past the present situation of living nations as they face the mounting menace of Militarism, and what he says about them is sharply alive and touches all of us to the quick. His comments are disturbing and are meant to disturb. The statesman, the soldier, the teacher, the pacifist—all are stirred to consider the question of War in a new light. Believing that nations like individuals can win salvation even at the eleventh hour and that the opportunity is open to them as long as life endures, Mr. Toynbee tells us 'we may and must pray that a reprieve which God has granted to our society once will not be refused if we ask for it again in a contrite spirit and with a broken heart.'

The high ground of Civilization which Mankind has won is again being swept by the scourge of Militarism because we still put our trust in the arts of War. There is higher ground ahead where, as Saint Paul assured the early Christians, 'though we walk in the flesh, we do not war after the flesh (for the weapons of our warfare are not carnal, but mighty through God to the pulling down of strong holds).' But there is also lower ground behind, and Mr. Toynbee realizes that if our society is unable to spiritualize its aggressive tendencies, it is better for it to practice the arts of War in the flesh rather than leave its house swept and empty for the invasion of even worse devils. Though he looks with the historian's unblinking eyes at all the horrors implicit and explicit in modern warfare, he sees that there is a social disintegration more to be feared than War itself, and if forced to choose between them, he would prefer War as the lesser evil.

Mr. Toynbee is aware, as few men can be, of the precariousness of our present plight in the desperate struggle against Militarism. He is fully conscious of the fact that only by winning the new ground ahead can we ultimately emerge victorious. But he is never so intent on the future that he does not keep an open eye on the past, never so preoccupied with the next step forward that he does not constantly bear in mind the danger of a misstep that will throw us back toward the chaotic past out of which civilized man has struggled. His insight into the hidden ways of man's being has convinced him that, should a nation or an individual attempt the new warfare whose weapons are not carnal before the necessary groundwork and training for it has been accomplished, that nation or individual would create a spiritual vacuum inviting a host of evils more terrible than the old warfare waged in the flesh. Armed as never before with a foreknowledge of the suicidal consequences of Militarism, the nations today have the means, Mr. Toynbee believes, to hold Militarism at bay until they work out a method of settling their conflicts without resort to War.

Albert V. Fowler

The contents of this small volume have been extracted, by
Mr. Albert Fowler, in consultation with the author, from the
first six comparatively large volumes of a work that will probably run to nine volumes of this larger size when the rest of it
is published. The extracts have been chosen to illustrate what
the writer of *A Study of History* has to say about War; and this
common subject gives them a unity; but the reader of the
present booklet is asked to bear in mind that here he will not
be reading these passages in their original context, and that
War is not the main theme of the work from which they have
been taken—though unhappily it is impossible to study the history of Mankind since the emergence, some five or six thousand years ago, of societies of the species known as civilizations without finding that the institution of War lies close
to the heart of this tragic subject.

In studying the breakdowns of civilizations, the writer has
indeed subscribed to the conclusion—no new discovery!—that
War has proved to have been the proximate cause of the
breakdown of every civilization which is known for certain
to have broken down, in so far as it has been possible to
analyze the nature of these breakdowns and to account for
their occurrence. There have been other sinister institutions
besides War with which Mankind has afflicted itself during its
age of Civilization; Slavery is one of these self-inflicted

scourges that leaps at once to our minds; yet, though Slavery, Caste, the Conflict of Classes, Economic Injustice, and many other social symptoms of the nemesis of Original Sin have played their part as instruments of Man's self-torment, War stands out among the rest as Man's principal engine of social and spiritual self-defeat during a period of his history which he is now beginning to be able to see in perspective.

A comparative survey of the known breakdowns of civilizations shows that social breakdown is a tragedy with a plot that has the institution of War for its key. Indeed War may actually have been a child of Civilization, since the possibility of waging war pre-supposes a minimum of technique and organization and surplus wealth beyond what is needed for bare subsistence, and these sinews of War were lacking to Primitive Man, while, on the other hand, we know of no civilization (with the possible exception of the Mayan, of which our knowledge up to date is only fragmentary) in whose life War has not been an established and dominant institution already at the earliest stage to which we can trace any civilization's history back.

Like other evils, War has an insidious way of appearing not intolerable until it has secured such a stranglehold upon the lives of its addicts that they no longer have the power to escape from its grip when its deadliness has become manifest. In the early stages of a civilization's growth, the cost of wars in suffering and destruction might seem to be exceeded by the benefits accruing from the winning of wealth and power and the cultivation of the 'military virtues'; and, in this phase of history, States have often found themselves able to indulge in War with one another with something like impunity even for the defeated party. War does not begin to reveal its malignity till the war-making society has begun to increase its economic ability to exploit Physical Nature and its political ability to organize 'man-power'; but, as soon as this happens, the God of War to which the growing society has long since been dedicated proves himself a Moloch by devouring an ever larger share of the increasing fruits of Man's industry and intelligence in the process of taking an ever larger toll of life and happiness; and, when the society's growth in efficiency reaches a point at which it becomes capable of mobilizing a lethal quantum of its energies and resources for military use, then War reveals itself as being a cancer which is bound to prove fatal to its victim unless he can cut it out and cast it from him, since its malignant tissues have now learnt to grow faster than the healthy tissues on which they feed.

In the past, when this danger-point in the history of the relations between War and Civilization has been reached and recognized, serious efforts have sometimes been made to get rid of War in time to save society, and these endeavours have been apt to take one or other of two alternative directions. Salvation cannot, of course, be sought anywhere except in the working of the consciences of individual human beings; but individuals have a choice between trying to achieve their aims through direct action as private persons and trying to achieve them through indirect action as citizens of States. A personal refusal to lend himself in any way to any war waged by his State for any purpose and in any circumstances is a line of attack against the institution of War that is likely to appeal to an ardent and self-sacrificing nature; by comparison, the alternative peace strategy of seeking to persuade and accustom Governments to combine in jointly resisting aggression when it comes and in trying to remove its stimuli beforehand may seem a circuitous and unheroic line of attack on the problem. Yet experience up to date indicates unmistakably, in the present writer's opinion, that the second of these two hard roads is by far the more promising.

The most obvious lion in the path of the strategy of Pacifism is the prospect which Pacifists have to face that, in so far as their action might prove effective, its first effect would be to put States in which Pacifism was an appreciably strong political force at the mercy of States in which it was impotent; and this would mean allowing the most unscrupulous Governments of the most benighted military Powers to make themselves masters of the World in the first chapter of the story. To face this prospect and submit to its immediate consequences pre-supposes an active foresight and a passive heroism that has been exhibited by saints but never by ordinary mankind in the mass. Peoples have, of course, frequently submitted *en masse* to the pain and grief of being oppressed by conquerors who have been brutal and barbarous by comparison with their victims. In A.D. 1940 the world came within an ace of thus submitting to the domination of a Germany controlled by the Nazis and inspired by Hitler's satanic spirit; but we have only to recall the temper prevalent in France and Great Britain during the years of 'appeasement' and thereafter in France in the era of Vichy to realize the truth that, among the motives inspiring a mass-refusal to resist military aggression by force of arms in self-defence, the Saint's unselfish horror of committing the sin of War is apt to count for much less than the ordinary mortal's natural aversion from being required to pay the awful price in blood and tears which War exacts.

A willingness to pay this price is the root of the so-called 'military virtues' without which War cannot be waged and, but for which, this evil institution would assuredly never have been condoned, as it has been till recently, by the public opinion and feeling of a majority of Mankind in societies in process of civilization. This traditional term 'military virtues' is, of course, misleading, since all virtues exhibited in war have

also an unlimited scope in other forms of human encounter
and intercourse, while, on the other hand, the exhibition of
these virtues by soldiers has unhappily often proved to be
compatible with a simultaneous exhibition of cruelty, rapacity,
and a host of further vices. In a contest of virtue between the
Warrior using violence and the Saint eschewing it, the Saint
would win a moral victory to-day which would bear practical
fruits tomorrow; but unfortunately the typical characters in
the drama of Pacifism versus War are not a Warrior and a
Saint both clad in the same panoply of righteousness; they are
the Warrior—virtuous or vicious—who has the courage to risk
life and limb, and the ordinary mortal who flinches from the
toil and danger; and, as we discovered for ourselves in A.D.
1939 and 1940, the unheroic character that is moved to shrink
from War by the common infirmity of human nature, and
not by the horror of committing a sin, had better try to rise
at any rate to the Warrior's level if he knows that the Saint's
altitude is beyond his reach.

By rising to the Warrior's level in the world wars of A.D.
1914–18 and A.D. 1939–45, unaggressive peoples did exercise the
cardinal virtues in War to such good effect that they twice defeated a militarist empire's long-prepared attempt to conquer
the World; and, in winning these successive victories at a fearful cost in blood and tears, they twice bought for our society
an opportunity to get rid of War by a better way than submission to a world-conqueror's forcibly imposed *Pax Oecumenica*. The first of these two opportunities was thrown away,
and the Second World War was our penalty for this flagrant
fault of heart and head. The second opportunity lies in our
hands to-day. Are we going to take it? What the situation
manifestly demands is a voluntary association of the peace-
loving peoples of the World in sufficient force and cohesion
to be unassailable by any who reject their pact of collective

security or who break it; and this peace-keeping world-power must not only be sufficiently preponderant in strength to make attacks upon it hopeless; it must also be sufficiently just and wise in the use of its power to avoid the provocation of any serious wish to challenge its authority.

This task, immense though it is, is not beyond our ability. Mankind's past successes in bringing once sovereign independent States into voluntary union with one another are guarantees that we possess the experience and technique for achieving the great work of political construction that is now demanded of us. We have the ability if we have the will. Our fate lies in our own hands.

London   *Arnold J. Toynbee*
June 1950

CONTENTS

Preface by Arnold J. Toynbee

I. The War-Stricken World of To-Day, 3

II. Militarism and the Military Virtues, 12

III. Sparta, the Military State, 26

IV. Assyria, the Strong Man Armed, 55

V. The Burden of Nineveh; Charlemagne and Timur Lenk, 78

VI. The Intoxication of Victory, 104

VII. Goliath and David, 112

VIII. The Price of Progress in Military Technique, 130

IX. The Failure of the Saviour with the Sword, 142

War and Civilization

————

CHAPTER I

The War-Stricken World of To-day

———

Unlike our forebears, we in our generation feel from the depths of our hearts that a *Pax Oecumenica* is now a crying need. We live in daily dread of a catastrophe which, we fear, may overtake us if the problem of meeting this need is left unsolved much longer. It would hardly be an exaggeration to say that the shadow of this fear that now lies athwart our future is hypnotizing us into a spiritual paralysis that is beginning to affect us even in the trivial avocations of our daily life. And, if we can screw up the courage to look this fear in the face, we shall not be rewarded by finding ourselves able to dismiss it with contempt as nothing but a panic phobia. The sting of this fear lies in the undeniable fact that it springs from a rational root.

We are terribly afraid of the immediate future because we have been through a horrible experience in the recent past. And the lesson which this experience has impressed upon our minds is indeed an appalling one. In our generation we have learnt, through suffering, two home truths. The first truth is that the institution of War is still in full force in our Western Society. The second truth is that, in the Western World under existing technical and social conditions, there can be no warfare that is not internecine. These truths have been driven home by our experience in the General Wars of A.D. 1914–18 and

1939–45; but the most ominous thing about these wars is that they were not isolated or unprecedented calamities. They were two wars in a series; and, when we envisage the whole series in a synoptic view, we discover that this is not only a series but also a progression. In our recent Western history war has been following war in an ascending order of intensity; and to-day it is already apparent that the War of 1939–45 was not the climax of this crescendo movement. If the series continues, the progression will indubitably be carried to ever higher terms, until this process of intensifying the horrors of war is one day brought to an end by the self-annihilation of the war-making society.

We may now remind ourselves that this progressive series of Western wars, of which the War of 1939–45 has been the latest but perhaps not the last, is one of two chapters of a story that we have already studied in another context. We have observed that the history of our Western warfare in the so-called 'Modern Age' can be analyzed into two bouts which are separated from one another chronologically by an intervening lull and are also distinguished from one another qualitatively by a difference in the object—or at any rate in the pretext—of the hostilities. The first bout consists of the Wars of Religion, which began in the sixteenth century and ceased in the seventeenth. The second bout consists of the Wars of Nationality, which began in the eighteenth century and are still the scourge of the twentieth. These ferocious Wars of Religion and ferocious Wars of Nationality have been separated by an interlude of moderate wars that were fought as 'the Sport of Kings.' This interlude manifestly did not begin on the Continent till after the end of the Thirty Years' War in A.D. 1648, and in Great Britain not till after the Restoration of the Monarchy in England in A.D. 1660; and it is equally manifest that the lull did not outlast the outbreak of the French Revolutionary War in A.D. 1792, even if we leave it an open question whether it survived the American Revolutionary War of A.D. 1775–83. On a narrower reckoning we might confine the Time-span of the 'Golden Age' of eighteenth-century moderation between the dates A.D. 1732 and A.D. 1755, if the eviction of a Protestant minority from the Catholic ecclesiastical principality of Salzburg in A.D. 1731–2 is to be taken as the last positive act of religious persecution in Western Europe, and the eviction of a French population from Acadia in A.D. 1755 as the first positive act of persecution for Nationality's sake in North America. In any case the interlude is palpable; and, whatever dates we may choose to adopt as the props for a conventional scheme of chronological demarcation, the play will fall into the same three acts in the same sequence, and this sequence of acts will present the same plot. This underlying plot, and not the superficial time-table, is the feature that is of interest for our present purpose. And in the plot of this three-act play, with its couple of bouts of ferocious warfare and an interlude of moderate warfare in between them, can we not discern the pattern of a couple of paroxysms, separated by a breathing-space, in which we may recognize the hall-mark of a 'Time of Troubles' following a breakdown? If we scrutinize in this light the picture that is presented by the modern history of our Western World, we shall find that the cap does at any rate fit to a nicety.

If the outbreak of the Wars of Religion in the sixteenth century is to be taken as a symptom of social breakdown, then the first rally of a since then disintegrating Western Society is to be seen in the movement in favour of religious toleration which gained the upper hand, and brought the Wars of Religion to an end, in the course of the seventeenth century. This victory of the Principle of Toleration in the religious sphere duly won for several succeeding generations that interlude of moderation which gave an ailing Western World a welcome breathing-space between a first and a second paroxysm of its deadly seizure. And the cap fits again when we observe the fact that the relief was only temporary and not permanent, and when we go on to inquire into the reason. For an empirical study of the rhythm of the disintegration-process leads us to expect to see a rally give way to a relapse; and it also leads us to expect to find that this monotonously repeated tale of failure can be explained in each case by some particular element of weakness by which the abortive rally has been vitiated. Are these expectations fulfilled in the Western case in point? We are bound to reply that, in this case too, the reason for the failure of the rally is as clear as the fact of it is conspicuous. Our modern Western Principle of Toleration has failed to bring salvation after all because (as we must confess) there has been no health in it. The spirits that presided over its conception and birth were Disillusionment, Apprehension and Cynicism, not Faith, Hope, and Charity; the impulse was negative, not positive; and the soil in which the seeds were sown was arid.

Some fell upon stony places where they had not much earth, and forthwith they sprung up because they had no deepness of earth; and when the Sun was up they were scorched, and because they had no root they withered away.

A Principle of Toleration which unexpectedly clothed the stony heart of our modern Western Christendom in a sudden crop of fresh verdure when the fierce sun of religious fanaticism had burnt itself out into dust and ashes, has wilted—no less suddenly and no less unexpectedly—now that the fiercer sun of national fanaticism has burst blazing through the firmament. In the twentieth century we are seeing our seventeenth-century Toleration making an unconditional surrender to a masterful demon whose onslaught it has proved incapable of withstanding. And the cause of this disastrous impotence is manifest.

A Toleration that has no roots in Faith has failed to retain any hold upon the heart of *Homo Occidentalis* because human nature abhors a spiritual vacuum. If the house from which an unclean spirit has gone out is left empty, swept, and garnished, the momentarily banished possessor will sooner or later enter in again with a retinue of other spirits more wicked than himself, and the last state of that man will be worse than the first. The Wars of Nationalism are more wicked than the Wars of Religion because the object—or pretext—of the hostilities is less sublime and less etherial. The moral is that hungry souls which have been given a stone when they have asked for bread cannot be restrained from seeking to satisfy their hunger by devouring the first piece of carrion that comes their way. They will not be deterred by a warning from the giver of the stone that the heaven-sent carrion is poisoned; and, even when the threatened agonies duly begin to wrack the miserable scavengers' entrails, they will persist in feasting upon the tainted meat with an unabated appetite until death extinguishes their greed —as once in Sicily a routed Athenian army that had gone mad with thirst as it walked through dry places, seeking rest and finding none, drank heedlessly of the waters of the River Asinarus while the enemy was shooting them down from the bank and the stream was running foully red with the blood of the dying drinkers' already slaughtered comrades.

There is yet another point in which our modern Western history conforms to the pattern of a disintegrating society's 'Time of Troubles'; and this is perhaps the most alarming of all these points of congruence. Our survey has shown us that, as a rule, the paroxysm which follows the intermediate breathing-space is more violent than the paroxysm which precedes it; and this rule is certainly exemplified in our Western case if the

Wars of Nationality are to be taken as the second paroxysm of our seizure and the Wars of Religion as the first.

Our forebears who fought that earlier cycle of ferocious Western wars may not have been behindhand in the will to work havoc, but—fortunately for themselves and for their descendants—they lacked the means which we now have at our command unfortunately for our children and for ourselves. No doubt the Wars of Religion were much worse—and this in point both of rancour and of command of resources and of technical ability to turn these resources to account—than the Western warfare of previous ages in which our Western Christendom was still unquestionably in growth. The Wars of Religion had been anticipated by the invention of gunpowder and by voyages of discovery that, at least on the material plane, had extended the range of the Western Society from one small corner of the Eurasian Continent to the hinterlands of all the navigable seas on the face of the planet. The bullion that had been accumulating in the treasuries at Tenochtitlan and Cuzco was ultimately expended on paying mercenaries to fight in the Wars of Religion on European battle-fields, after the discovery, conquest, and rifling of the Central American and Andean worlds by the Spanish *conquistadores*—just as, after the corresponding geographical expansion of the Hellenic World through the exploits of Alexander, the treasures piled up by Achaemenian policy at Ecbatana and Susa found their way into the hands of mercenaries who fought in the wars of Alexander's diadochi and epigoni on battle-fields in Greece. And the professional soldiery that was maintained in a sixteenth-century and seventeenth-century Western World out of this sudden huge increase in the Western princes' supplies of the precious metals was not only more numerous than the old feudal militia of Transalpine Western Europe. It was also more formidably armed and, worse still, more ferociously en-

raged against an enemy who now, as a rule, was not only a
military opponent but was also a religious miscreant in the eyes
of his adversary. The unprecedented violence with which the
Wars of Religion were imbued by the combined operation of
these several causes would doubtless have shocked both Saint
Louis and the Emperor Frederick II if they could have returned to life to witness the Western warfare of the sixteenth
and seventeenth centuries. But we may also as confidently pre-
sume that the Duke of Alva and Gustavus Adolphus would
have been shocked to an equal degree if they, in their turn,
could have returned to life to witness the subsequent Wars of
Nationality. This later cycle of ferocious Western wars which
began in the eighteenth century, and which has not ceased in
the twentieth, has been keyed up to an unprecedented degree of ferocity by the titanic driving-power of two forces—
Democracy and Industrialism—which have entered into the
institution of War in our Western World in these latter days
when that world has now virtually completed its stupendous
feat of incorporating the whole face of the Earth and the
entire living generation of Mankind into its own body material. Our last state is worse than our first because, in this vastly
expanded house, we are possessed to-day by devils more terrible
than any that ever tormented even our seventeenth-century and
sixteenth-century ancestors.

Are these devils to dwell in our empty and swept and garnished house till they have driven us to suicide? If the analogy
between our Western Civilization's modern history and other
civilizations' 'Times of Troubles' does extend to points of
chronology, then a Western 'Time of Troubles' which appears to have begun sometime in the sixteenth century may be
expected to find its end sometime in the twentieth century;
and this prospect may well make us tremble; for in other cases
the grand finale that has wound up a 'Time of Troubles' and

ushered in a universal state has been a self-inflicted 'knock-out blow' from which the self-stricken society has never been able to recover. Must we, too, purchase our *Pax Oecumenica* at this deadly price? The question is one which our own lips cannot answer, since the destiny of a live civilization is necessarily as obscure to its living members as the fate of a dead civilization is to scholars when their only clues are undeciphered scripts or dumb artifacts. We cannot say for certain that our doom is at hand; and yet we have no warrant for assuming that it is not; for that would be to assume that we are not as other men are; and any such assumption would be at variance with everything that we know about human nature either by looking around us or by introspection.

This dark doubt is a challenge which we cannot evade; and our destiny depends on our response.

I dreamed, and behold I saw a man cloathed with rags, standing in a certain place, with his face from his own house, a book in his hand, and a great burden upon his back. I looked, and saw him open the book and read therein; and as he read he wept and trembled; and, not being able longer to contain, he broke out with a lamentable cry saying 'What shall I do?'

It was not without just cause that Christian was so greatly distressed.

I am for certain informed [said he] that this our city will be burned with fire from Heaven—in which fearful overthrow both myself with thee my wife and you my sweet babes shall miserably come to ruine, except (the which yet I see not) some way of escape can be found, whereby we may be delivered.

What response to this challenge is Christian going to make? Is he going to look this way and that way as if he would run, yet stand still because he cannot tell which way to go—until the fire from Heaven duly descends upon the City of Destruction and the wretched haverer perishes in a holocaust which he has so dismally foreboded without ever bringing himself to the point of fleeing from the wrath to come? Or will he begin to run—and run on crying 'Life! Life! Eternal Life!'—with his eye set on a shining light and his feet bound for a distant wicket-gate? If the answer to this question depended on nobody but Christian himself, our knowledge of the uniformity of human nature might incline us to predict that Christian's imminent destiny was Death and not Life. But in the classic version of the myth we are told that the human protagonist was not left entirely to his own resources in the hour that was decisive for his fate. According to John Bunyan, Christian was saved by his encounter with Evangelist. And, inasmuch as it cannot be supposed that God's nature is less constant than Man's, we may and must pray that a reprieve which God has granted to our society once will not be refused if we ask for it again in a contrite spirit and with a broken heart.

CHAPTER II

Militarism and the Military Virtues

That Militarism is suicidal is a proposition which will hardly be disputed by any one whose opinion carries weight; but, if this proposition is almost a truism, then it is unlikely to offer a solution of the moral problem that is presented by the institution of War; and, in fact, the word Militarism in itself implies that this suicidal and iniquitous way of using military force is not the only way, but is rather a perversion—for which we have to coin a special name—of an institution which is not proved to be evil in its essence, *ipso facto*, by the admission that it lends itself to a monstrous abuse.

Is War intrinsically and irredeemably evil in itself? This is a question which cannot be shirked by any student of history or by any member of our Western Society in our generation, when it is the crucial question on which the destiny of our civilization hangs. The time has come when we must grapple with it; but, before we come to grips, we must make sure that we are taking account of all the difficulties.

The grand difficulty, of course, is the evident existence and importance of 'the military virtues.' These confront us as a monumental fact which cannot be whittled down or explained away. It is one of the commonplaces of popular sociological observation that the military peoples, castes, and classes are apt to win more admiration from us than their neighbours who

earn their living by occupations which do not entail the risking
of one's own life in the attempt to take some one else's. There
is, indeed, an old-fashioned type of English military or naval
officer—nice in his sense of honour, considerate to his fellow
human beings, and kind to animals (though he enjoys killing
them for sport!)—who has been regarded, for at least two centuries past, as one of the finest English products of our Western Christian Civilization. Nor can this admiration be dismissed
with contempt as being naïve or snobbish. If we look into it
seriously and with no *parti pris*, we shall assuredly be confirmed in our belief that it is deserved. For 'the military virtues' are not in a class apart; they are virtues which are virtues
in every walk of life. Courage, which is the most prominent of
them, is a cardinal virtue in every action to which a human
being can set his hand—or hers; and the other virtues which
we have ascribed to our legendary colonel or commodore are
also patently legal tender in civil as well as in military life.
Colonel Newcome and the Chevalier Bayard; Cœur-de-Lion
and Roland; Olaf Tryggvason and Siegfried; Regulus and
Leonidas; Partāp Singh and Prithīrāj; Jalāl-ad-Dīn Manko-
birnī and 'Abdallah al-Battāl; Yoshitsune Minamoto and Kuang
Yü: what a goodly company they are, and how large a place
they fill in the historical landscape of these last five or six
thousand years within which Mankind has embarked upon the
enterprise of Civilization!

What are we to make of the vein in our social tradition
which till yesterday was still inspiring heroes such as these and
which to-day still moves the rest of us to admire them? If we
wish to understand either the value of 'the military virtues' or
the sincerity of the admiration which they win, we must take
care to look at them in their native social setting; and one feature of this which is pertinent to our present inquiry leaps
readily to the eye. 'The military virtues' are cultivated and ad-

mired in a milieu in which social forces are not sharply distinguished in people's minds from the non-human natural forces,
and in which it is at the same time taken for granted that natural forces are not amenable to human control.

Down to modern times, War was almost universally regarded as
something which in itself required no justification. Its drawbacks
and horrors were, indeed, recognized, but at worst it was considered an inevitable evil, a calamity, a scourge sent by God, of the
same unavoidable nature as the plague. To a community threatened
by Vikings, or other aggressive neighbours, this was the obvious
way to regard it. From the victim's point of view there *was* no distinction in principle between the sudden incursions of such people
and those of a horde of locusts or a cloud of disease germs. But this
made it all the more natural to admire and honour the prowess of
an Alfred or a Charlemagne, who could protect his people from
disaster in such circumstances. Down to modern times, though the
justification for a particular war might be questioned, and its hard-
ship realized, fighting was all in the day's work, an incident of human existence the abolition of which was hardly an imaginable possibility. In these circumstances, while few may have praised war,
everyone valued the warrior, and submitted willingly to his leadership and control. Down to the nineteenth century the army was
regarded as almost the only profession open to a gentleman, and a
gentleman is 'armiger.' [1]

The gentleman and scholar who has communicated these
observations to the writer of this volume goes on, in the course
of the same letter, to make an illuminating comparison between
War and 'Sport.'

In prehistoric times, before the domestication of animals, the
hunter discharged a very necessary function in providing food.
Surrounded by raiding barbarians, the soldier equally served to
make life more tolerable and justice more capable of attainment. The
finest men attached themselves to these pursuits, and their achieve-

[1] Mr. G. M. Gathorne-Hardy in a letter to the present writer.

ments were rightly honoured, and the same type of man tends to inherit their instincts with their qualities. But their functions have become less necessary; in the case of the hunter, perhaps, entirely useless.

The comparison is illuminating because, in the case of hunting, we see a pursuit which, at a primitive level of life, has been socially valuable and even vitally necessary becoming unquestionably superfluous at an early, and a frequently attained, stage of economic advance. At this stage the practice of hunting for a livelihood becomes transformed, perhaps usually by a gradual process of change, into an economically otiose 'sport.' On this analogy, can we posit a stage of social progress at which the practice of War in sheer self-defence against uncontrollable hostile forces becomes comparably transformed into a socially otiose Militarism? On this analogy the sinister Militarism which we can distinguish empirically from the innocent prowess of the happy warrior might perhaps be defined as a practice of War for War's sake when the institution has ceased both to be, and to be regarded as being, a social necessity.

In our Western World in the so-called 'modern' chapter of its history we have seen War placed on the same shelf as hunting during an eighteenth-century 'lull' when War was only in vogue as 'the sport of kings.' The bad name of militarist, which glances off the armour of a Cœur-de-Lion or a Bayard, is a Devil's cockade which sticks fast in the *tricorne* of a Charles XII or a Frederick the Great. The kings who took their sport on the Western battle-fields of that age were militarists beyond question. Yet, in the light of our later experience, it has to be said in their favour that Frederick and his kind were not the most pernicious exponents of Militarism that were to afflict our modern Western Society. Frederick, for example, would never have dreamed of glorifying War as it has been glorified in a classic passage from the pen of a later Prussian militarist, Hellmuth von Moltke.

Perpetual Peace is a dream—and not even a beautiful dream—and War is an integral part [*ein Glied*] of God's ordering of the Universe [*Weltordnung*]. In War, Man's noblest virtues come into play [*entfalten sich*]: courage and renunciation, fidelity to duty and a readiness for sacrifice that does not stop short of offering up Life itself. Without War the World would become swamped in materialism.

In this extravagant eulogy of War there is a note of passion, of anxiety and of rancour which is a far cry from the urbane and philosophic scepticism of a Frederick the Great. So profound a change of tone is presumably the echo of comparably profound changes of temper and circumstance which had come over the Western World within the period of less than a hundred years that had elapsed between Frederick's death in A.D. 1786 and the year in which von Moltke wrote this letter to Bluntschli. We can observe two such changes which are of this magnitude.

By the time when our nineteenth-century Prussian militarist was an old man, the eighteenth-century cultivation of War as 'the sport of kings' had, in fact, evoked two reactions which were not only distinct but were antithetical. Both reactions proceeded from the common postulate that to fight for fun was shocking; but, while one school of reformers took the line that an evil which had been turned into a sport both could and should be abolished altogether, the other took the line that the evil could not be borne if it were not to be endured for a serious purpose. Thus, when the royal sportsmanship of the eighteenth century fell into a unanimous discredit, the nineteenth-century pacifists found themselves confronted by a nineteenth-century brood of militarists of von Moltke's type who were far more formidable than their frivolous eighteenth-century predecessors.

This quarrel over the reform of an eighteenth-century abuse between two opposing parties of nineteenth-century 'progressives' perhaps accounts for von Moltke's tone in the passage that we have quoted. In this *extravaganza* he is bidding defiance to contemporary pacifists.

It is when an institution no longer appears necessary, that fantastic reasons are sought or invented for satisfying the instinctive prejudice in its favour, which its long persistence has created. It is just the same with the sport of the hunter; you will find its most elaborate defence in very recent literature, precisely because what is now challenged was at an earlier period taken for granted.[2]

In this contest between the pacifist who seeks to abolish 'the sport of kings' and the militarist who seeks to reconvert it into a serious business of the peoples, what are the omens to-day? We can hardly forbear to ask a question which may be the riddle of our Society's destiny; but the omens, as far as we can read them, are not at present reassuring. In our own day we have seen von Moltke's provocative thesis adopted as one of the fundamental articles of their creed by the prophets of Fascism and Naziism, and accepted with enthusiasm by the masses whom these prophets have succeeded in converting to their faith.

Signor Mussolini defined a Fascist militarist's faith on two separate occasions. Speaking at the close of the Italian army manœuvres in 1934, he said: 'We are becoming—and shall become so increasingly, because this is our desire—a military nation. A militaristic nation, I will add, since we are not afraid of words. To complete this picture: warlike—that is to say, endowed ever to a higher degree with the virtues of obedience,

[2] Mr. G. M. Gathorne-Hardy, in the letter quoted above.

sacrifice, and dedication to country.' And in an article in the *Enciclopedia Italiana*, on 'The Doctrine of Fascism,' he wrote: 'War alone brings all human energies to their highest tension and sets a seal of nobility on the peoples who have the virtue to face it.'

This so-called 'heroic' attitude towards life is being welcomed with open arms, and taken in deadly earnest, at this moment by millions of young men, and the reason why it appeals to them is manifest. They are greedy for the virtues in the form of 'the military virtues' because they have been starved of other kinds of spiritual bread, like the Prodigal Son who, when starved of human food, 'would fain have filled his belly with the husks that the swine did eat.' Moreover we know what these prodigals' spiritual sustenance used to be, and when their starvation began. These latter-day Western worshippers of 'the military virtues' are the epigoni of generations which were nurtured in 'the Christian virtues'; and they began to be starved of the traditional Christian morality, upon which their forebears had been brought up, when, at the turn of the eighteenth and nineteenth centuries, the unbelief of a cultivated minority in the Western World began to infect the less sophisticated masses.

The truth is that the spirit of Man abhors a spiritual vacuum; and, if a human being, or a human society, has the tragic misfortune to lose a sublime inspiration by which it has once been possessed, then, sooner or later, it will seize upon any other spiritual food that it can find—however coarse and unsatisfying this new fodder may be—rather than remain without any spiritual sustenance at all. In the light of this truth the recent spiritual history of our Western Society can be told—and the glorification of War can be explained—as follows: Owing to the breakdown of the Hildebrandine Papacy, which was the master-institution of our medieval Western Christendom, our

Western *Plebs Christiana* received such a grievous moral shock
that the Christian way of life, in which our forebears had been
brought up, very largely lost its hold upon us; and, finding
ourselves, at the end of a series of calamities and disillusion-
ments, with our house swept and garnished by an intellectual
Aufklärung, but untenanted by the Christian spirit that had
formerly dwelt in it, we cast about for other tenants to fill an
agonizing spiritual void. In this search we addressed ourselves
to the alternatives that lay nearest to our hand. Our Western
culture had three sources—namely, the internal proletariat and
the external proletariat and the dominant minority of the Hellenic Society to which our Western Society was 'affiliated'—
and when Christianity, which was the religious legacy of the
Hellenic internal proletariat, appeared to fail us we turned hun-
grily to the religions of the Hellenic external proletariat and
the Hellenic dominant minority. As it happened, these two
religions were virtually the same; they were, both of them,
variants of the primitive idolatrous worship of the tribe or
state; and therefore the modern Western apostate from Christianity, in his search after a new god, found the same idol
awaiting his adoration in whichever of the two alternative
directions he cast his eyes. Machiavelli consulting his Livy and
Rousseau his Plutarch and De Gobineau his Sturlason and
Hitler his Wagner were each led, by his respective literary or
musical oracle, to the altar-steps of the same Abomination of
Desolation: the Totalitarian Parochial State. In this pagan worship of the parochial community—be it Hellenic or Gothic or
Scandinavian in its inspiration—the cult of 'the military virtues'
is an obligatory practice, and the glorification of War a fundamental article of faith. And we can now understand why
von Moltke exclaims, with a passion which is assuredly sincere,
that 'Perpetual Peace is not even a beautiful dream,' and why
he deprecates the abolition of War in a fear, which is mani-

festly genuine, lest the realization of the pacifist's dream may
simply plunge our neo-pagan world back again into a spiritual
vacuum.

In fact, we may be driven to admit that von Moltke is right
in taking this stand if he is right in his underlying assumption
that modern Western Man is confined to a choice between two,
and only two, alternatives. If we have really lost the power or
the will to practise the virtues of Gethsemane, then it is certainly better to practise those of Sparta or Valhalla than to
practise none at all. And in a *ci-devant* Christian society this
conclusion is no longer academic; for, in turning our condi-
tional clause into the simple indicative, von Moltke is now being followed by the masses; and his disciples in our generation
can claim, without fear of contradiction, that they have the
big battalions on their side. The latter-day Western cult of 'the
military virtues' as the Ten Commandments of a Totalitarian
Parochial State is fast becoming the prevalent religion of the
age; and this faith, archaistically barbaric though it be, will
never be overcome by the Mephistophelian spirit of sheer
negation against which it is itself a victorious protest. Societies
are apt to get the religions, as well as the governments, that
they deserve; and, if we have become unworthy of our Christian birthright, then we have condemned ourselves to worship
the resuscitated ghost of an Odin or an Ares. This barbaric
faith is better than none at all; in the deaths of a Leonidas and
an Olaf Tryggvason the heroism which Militarism inculcates
has risen to the height of sublimity; but this is not the sublimity
of the saints, and not a heroism which leads anywhere except
to suicide. Witness the fates of the abortive Scandinavian Civilization and the arrested Spartan Civilization. And such will
likewise be the fate of our Western Civilization if von Moltke
is right in his underlying assumption of fact, as well as in his
moral deduction from it. It remains to be seen whether this

assumption is correct, or whether on the other hand Christianity, so far from being out of the running, has still the power to release the soul of *Homo Occidentalis* from the grip of a hideous and destructive paganism by offering him, once more, a higher positive alternative. Can Hildebrand arise again in his might to heal the wounds inflicted upon the souls of his flock by the sins of a Rodrigo Borgia and a Sinibaldo Fieschi? This is the greatest of all the questions that have to be answered in our Western World in this twentieth century.

In following the clue that has been given us by von Moltke, and examining the hold which the worship of 'the military virtues' has been reacquiring over our Western souls in these latter days, we may find that we have made some progress towards solving our problem of whether the institution of War is intrinsically and irredeemably evil in itself. We have discovered, in effect, that the problem has been wrongly propounded. Perhaps the truth is that no created thing can ever be evil intrinsically and irredeemably, because no created thing is incapable of serving as a vehicle for the virtues that flow from the Creator. 'The military virtues' are virtues none the less for being jewels set in blood and iron; but the value lies in the jewels themselves and not in their horrible setting; and it is flying in the face of all experience to jump to the conclusion that the only place where we can ever hope to find these precious things is the slaughterhouse where they have happened to make their first epiphany to human eyes. The diamond that is secreted in the clay does not remain there, but finds a fitter setting in the crown of a king; and when once the diamond-mine has yielded up its treasure it ceases to be anything but a death-trap for the miner who cannot now tear himself away from the scene of his habitual toil and his accidental trove. What is true of the dross in which the diamond has lain buried is likewise true of the ephemeral institution of War in which an eternal principle of goodness has glimmered darkly for a season, in the guise of 'the military virtues,' in order that it may shine out brightly hereafter in the perfect physical peace of the City of God. It is the divine virtue—unchanging in itself, but always changing its temporal abode—that casts the reflection of its own inner light upon each of its successive dwelling-places; and each of these dwelling-places assumes a derelict ugliness as soon as the temporarily indwelling spirit has ceased to lighten its darkness.

There is hardly any occurrence or phenomenon about which we need always be of the same mind if we trace it back through the ages. That is, no evil was originally an evil, but only became so . . . Many . . . instances of things originally good, but which have outlived their purpose, could be quoted; and among them perhaps we might include War. Like everything which has life, War never remains stationary, but is always developing. Animals did not wage war, but human beings did, and our descendants—the 'supermen,' as Goethe and Nietzsche call them—will cease to do so . . . The [institution of] War, with which history has acquainted us, was once born; it was young and now is old. But, just as the love of a maid seems to us lovely and that of an old woman repulsive, even so it is with War: we cannot and must not judge alike two things which from their very nature and meaning are wholly different. There is nothing whatever in common between Achilles' eternal Song of Hate and Lissauer's Hymn of Hate to England; and similarly there is the profoundest difference between the battles in the Scamander Valley and the fighting between the Meuse and the Moselle.[3]

If we have persisted in the worship of War when the goodness which once found a genuine though inadequate expression in 'the military virtues' has been given an incomparably higher sphere for its exercise in the Christian life, then we have been guilty of that idolization of an ephemeral institution which is

[3] Nicolai, G. F.: *The Biology of War*, English translation, pp. 420-21.

one form of the nemesis of creativity. And our sin is aggravated if, after centuries spent in attempting the impossible feat of serving two masters, we have latterly held to the lower and despised the higher—relapsing altogether into the service of Odin and Ares, and repudiating even that half-hearted service which was rendered to Christ by our forebears. This last state of paganism is vastly worse than the first; for the deliberate and self-conscious perversity of von Moltke's and Mussolini's archaistic Militarism is as different from the innocently archaic 'military virtues' of the Chevalier Bayard and Colonel Newcome as the dusk of evening is different from the gleam of dawn. The innocence which the Colonel inherited from the Chevalier can never be recaptured in our Western World by the heirs of Frederick's and Napoleon's cynicism. Colonel Newcome's own author was well aware, when he created this lovable character in the middle of the nineteenth century, that his creature's charm and tragedy both owed something to the fact of his being already an anachronism. The devotees of a Mussolinian Mars Redivivus will not be Newcomes or Bayards; they will be Robots and Martians. This process of perversion, which is the Dead Sea fruit of an Idolatry mated with Archaism, is the exact reverse of that process of 'etherialization,' and that progressive transference of the field of action from the Macrocosm to the Microcosm, in which we may find a criterion of growth. If this criterion is the true one, it informs us *a priori* that the institution of War cannot be morally static. Granting that this gruesome institution has provided a field for the exercise of 'the military virtues' yesterday, we may be sure that to-morrow the 'chivalrous' kind of War will either rankle into a Militarism without a vestige of virtue or beauty or else will be transfigured into a *militia Christi* in which the physical warfare of one man against another will have been

translated into a spiritual warfare of all men united in the service of God against the powers of evil.

If our present apostasy proves only to be the last convulsion
of a paganism *in articulo mortis,* and if this supreme crisis in
the long-drawn-out struggle between paganism and Christianity is to end in paganism being driven completely off the field,
we may dream of an age to come in which Physical War will
have passed out of our life and faded out of our memory until
the very word 'war' loses currency—as the kindred word 'sacrifice' has lost it already—except in a meaning which was originally a metaphor. In those days, when men speak of 'war,'
they will be referring to the war of the spirit; and, if they are
ever reminded of the physical warfare which was the constant
scourge of their predecessors for some six or seven thousand
years, they will think of it in the category of one of those
cruel initiation rites to which *Homo Catechumenus* used to
submit himself in order to win his way at last into a Com-
munion of Saints in which the theatre of War has been transferred from an outward to an inward battle-field. The warfare
of that perfect *Respublica Christiana* has been depicted with
a poetic wealth of military imagery, and has been described
with the prophetic vision of sainthood, by one of its citizens
who came to proclaim the advent of the *Civitas Dei* many hun-
dreds or thousands of years in advance. Saint Paul was delivering his message to the citizens of the war-stricken cities of a
Hellenic universal state in an age of Hellenic history when the
gleam of 'the military virtues' could still catch and captivate
the eye from beneath the tarnish deposited by the Militarism
of a 'Time of Troubles'; and the Apostle seizes upon all the
noble and glorious connotations of War that still survive in his
converts' minds in order to convey to them, in a chain of military metaphors, the more etherial glory and nobility of the
Christian life.

Though we walk in the flesh, we do not war after the flesh (for the weapons of our warfare are not carnal, but mighty through God to the pulling down of strong holds): casting down imaginations, and every high thing that exalteth itself against the knowledge of God, and bringing into captivity every thought to the obedience of Christ.

CHAPTER III

Sparta, the Military State

When Plato conceived his Utopia, he was inspired by the actual institutions of the Spartan city-state: a Hellenic community which was the greatest among the Great Powers of the Hellenic World in Plato's day. When we look into the origins of the Spartan system, we find that the Spartans were confronted with the necessity of performing their *tour de force*, and equipping themselves for the task with their 'peculiar institution,' because, at an earlier stage in the course of their history, they had taken a peculiar turning. The Spartans parted company, at a certain point in their history, from the common run of Hellenic city-state communities.

The Spartans made a peculiar response to the common challenge which was presented to all Hellenic communities in the eighth century B.C., when, in consequence of the immediately antecedent course of Hellenic social development, the extension of the area under cultivation in the homelands of the Hellenic Society in Peninsular Greece and in the Archipelago had begun to bring in diminishing returns while the population of Hellas was rapidly increasing in numbers. The 'normal' solution which was found for this common problem of eighth-century Hellenic life was the further extension of the total arable area in Hellenic hands by the discovery and conquest of new territories overseas. In the galaxy of new Hellenic city-states that came into existence as a result of this general movement of overseas expansion, there was one foundation, Tarentum, which claimed a Spartan origin; but, even if this claim was in accordance with historical fact, the case of Tarentum was unique. Tarentum was the only Hellenic city overseas which even purported to be a Spartan colony; and this Tarentine tradition merely points the truth that, in the main, the Spartans sought to solve the common eighth-century Hellenic population-problem, not along the common lines of overseas colonization, but in their own peculiar way.

When the Spartans found even their broad and fertile ploughlands in the vale of the Eurotas too narrow for a growing population, they did not turn their eyes to the sea, like the Chalcidians or Corinthians or Megarians. The sea is not visible either from Sparta city or from any point on the Spartan plain or even from the heights that immediately surround it. The natural feature which dominates the Spartan landscape is the towering mountain-range of Taygetus, which rises so sheer from the western edge of the plain that its face seems almost perpendicular, while its line is so straight and so continuous that it gives the impression of a wall. This wall-like aspect of Taygetus attracts the eye to the Langádha: a gorge which cleaves the range at right angles as though the titanic architect of plain and mountain had expressly designed this one apparent break in an otherwise uniformly impassable barrier in order to provide his people with a sally-port. When the Spartans began, in the eighth century B.C., to feel the pinch of population-pressure, they lifted up their eyes unto the hills and beheld the Langádha and sought their help in the pass through the mountains, as their neighbours, under the same spur of Necessity, were seeking theirs in the passage over the sea. At this first parting of the ways, help did come to the Spartans from the lord Apollo of Amyclae and the lady Athana of the Brazen

House. The First Messeno-Spartan War (*circa* 736–720 B.C.), which was contemporary with the first Hellenic settlements on the Thracian and Sicilian coasts, left the Spartan victors in possession of broader conquered lands in Hellas than the Chalcidian colonists won overseas at Leontini or the Spartans' own reputed colonists at Tarentum. But the Presiding Genius of Sparta, who led her and who did 'not suffer' her 'foot to be moved' when once she had reached her Messenian goal, did not thereby 'preserve' her 'from all evil.' On the contrary, the superhuman—or inhuman—fixity of Sparta's subsequent posture, like the mythical doom of Lot's wife, was manifestly a curse and not a blessing.

The Spartans' peculiar troubles began as soon as the First Messeno-Spartan War had ended in a Spartan victory; for to conquer the Messenians in war was a less difficult task for the Spartans than to hold them down in peace-time. These conquered Messenians were no barbarous Thracians or Sikels, but Hellenes of like culture, and like passions, with the Spartans themselves: all but their equals in war and perhaps more than their equals in numbers. The First Messeno-Spartan War (*circa* 736–720 B.C.) was child's-play compared to the Second (*circa* 650–620 B.C.), in which the subject Messenians—tempered by adversity and filled with shame and rage at having submitted to a fate by which no other Hellenes had allowed themselves to be overtaken—now rose in arms against their Spartan rulers and fought far harder and longer, in this second bout, to recover their freedom than they had fought in the first bout to preserve it. Their tardy heroism failed, in the end, to avert a second Spartan victory; and, after this unprecedentedly stubborn and exhausting war, the victors treated the vanquished with unprecedented severity. Yet, in the long view of the Gods, the Messenian insurgents had secured their revenge on Sparta, in the sense in which Hannibal was to have his revenge on Rome. The Second Messeno-Spartan War changed the whole rhythm of Spartan life and deflected the whole course of Spartan history. It was one of those wars in which the iron enters into the survivors' souls. It was so terrible an experience that it left Spartan life fast bound in misery and iron, and it 'side-tracked' Spartan evolution into a blind alley. And since the Spartans were never able to forget what they had gone through, they were never able to relax, and therefore never able to extricate themselves from the impasse of their post-war reaction.

The relations of the Spartans with their human environment in Messenia passed through the same ironic vicissitudes as the relations of the Esquimaux with their physical environment in the Arctic Zone. In either case we have the spectacle of a community which ventures to grapple with an environment that daunts this community's neighbours, in order to wring from this excessively formidable enterprise an exceptionally rich reward. In the first phase, this act of audacity seems to be justified by results. The Esquimaux find better hunting on the Arctic ice than their less adventurous Indian cousins can find on the North American prairies; the Spartans, in the First Messeno-Spartan War, win richer lands from their fellow-Hellenes across the mountains than the contemporary Chalcidian colonists can win from barbarians across the sea. But in the next phase the original—and irrevocable—act of audacity brings its ineluctable penalty. The conquered environment now takes its audacious conqueror captive. The Esquimaux become prisoners of the Arctic climate and have to shape their lives according to its exacting dictates down to the smallest detail. The Spartans, having conquered Messenia in the First War in order to live unto themselves, are constrained, in the Second War and ever after, to give up their lives to the task of keeping Messenia. They live as the obedient humble servants of their own dominion over Messenia from this time forth for ever-more.

The Spartans equipped themselves for performing their *tour de force* by adapting existing institutions to fulfil new needs.

The way . . . in which those primitive institutions, which other-wise vanished in all Greek communities before the face of the ris-ing [Hellenic] culture, were made to serve as the corner-stones of the Spartan organism, is something which exacts from us the deep-est admiration.

In this adaptation, one cannot refuse to discern something which is more than the mere result of an automatic development. The methodical and purposeful way in which everything has been made to lead towards one single goal forces us to see here the interven-tion of a consciously shaping hand . . . The existence of one man, or of several men working in the same direction, who have remod-elled the primitive institutions into the *Agôgê* and the *Kosmos*, is a necessary hypothesis.[1]

Hellenic tradition attributed not only the reconstruction of the Lacedaemonian Society after the Second Messeno-Spartan War—a reconstruction which made Sparta what she was and what she remained ever after until she collapsed—but also all the antecedent and less abnormal events in Spartan social and political history to 'Lycurgus.' But 'Lycurgus' was a god; and modern Western scholars, in search for a human author of the 'Lycurgean' system, have been inclined to find their man in Chilon, a Spartan Overseer who left a reputation as a sage and who appears to have held office about 550 B.C. Perhaps we shall not go far wrong if we regard the 'Lycurgean' system as the cumulative work of a series of Spartan statesmen during some-thing like a century, dating from the outbreak of the Second Messeno-Spartan War.

[1] Nilsson, M. P.: 'Die Grundlagen des Spartanischen Lebens,' in *Klio*, vol. xii, p. 308.

In the Spartan system the outstanding feature—the feature which accounts alike for the system's astonishing efficiency and for its fatal rigidity and for its consequent breakdown—was its 'grand disregard for human nature.' Virtually the whole burden of maintaining the Spartan dominion over Messenia was imposed on the free-born children of free-born Spartiates. At the same time, within the Spartiate citizen-body itself, the principle of equality was not only well-established but was carried to great lengths.

Though there was not an equalization of wealth, every Spartiate 'Peer' held from the State one of the fiefs or allotments of equal magnitude—or equal productivity—into which the arable land of Messenia had been divided up after the Second Messeno-Spartan War; and each of these allotments, which was cultivated by the labour of Messenians bound to the soil as serfs, was calculated to support a Spartiate 'Peer' and his family, on a 'spartanly' frugal standard of living, without their having to labour with their own hands. Accordingly, every Spartiate 'Peer,' however poor, was economically in a position to devote his whole time and energy to the art of war; and since permanent and perpetual military training and service were also incumbent upon every Spartiate 'Peer,' however rich he might be, the residual inequality of wealth was not, at Sparta, reflected in any substantial difference between the rich man's and the poor man's way of life.

In the matter of hereditary rank, the Spartan nobility appear to have retained no political privilege denied to commoners except eligibility to the Council of State. For the rest, they were absorbed into the rank and file of the 'Peers'; and, in particular, the three hundred knights of Sparta were no longer, under the 'Lycurgean' system, either a club of nobles or a mounted force. They had become a *corps d'élite* of heavy infantrymen which was recruited by merit from all the 'Peers,'

who competed eagerly for admission. The most striking mani-
festation of the equalitarian spirit of the 'Lycurgean' system
was the status to which it reduced the Kings. Though the
Kings continued to succeed to the throne by hereditary right,
the one substantial power which they retained was the military command on active service. Otherwise, apart from certain ceremonial duties and privileges which were less important
than picturesque, the reigning Kings, as well as all other members of the two royal families, had to submit to the same exacting and life-long discipline as ordinary 'Peers.' As heirs apparent, they received the same education; and their succession to
the throne brought them no exemption.

Thus, within the fraternity of the Spartiate 'Peers,' differ-
ences of birth and of hereditary privilege counted, under the
'Lycurgean' system, for little or nothing; and, although one
normal qualification for admission into this fraternity was free
Spartiate birth, no candidates for admission would ever have
dreamt of saying—even within themselves, let alone in public
—the Spartan equivalent of 'We have Abraham to our father';
for Spartiate birth was no guarantee of promotion to the cov-
eted though onerous status of a 'Peer.' Indeed, Spartiate birth,
though normally required, was not a *sine qua non*. Spartiate
birth simply condemned a child (if it were not reprieved by
being rejected as a weakling after birth and put out to die of
exposure) to undergo the ordeal of a Spartan education; and
this ordeal merely entitled a boy to compete for a place in the
fraternity of the 'Peers' when he came of age. A child's response to this ordeal of education counted for more than his
birth in the last resort. There were Spartiates born who failed
to give satisfaction under the educational test and who were
therefore eventually refused admission to the fraternity of
'Peers' and were left to weep and gnash their teeth in outer
darkness in the unenviable status of 'Inferiors.' Conversely,

there were cases—though these were evidently rare—in which non-Spartiate boys were allowed to undergo the Spartan education; and if these 'Alien Boys' acquitted themselves well, they appear to have been no less eligible for enrolment among the 'Peers' than their Spartiate class-mates.

To this extent the Spartan system ignored the claims of birth and heredity, and the God Lycurgus went still farther in defiance of 'human nature.' The Spartan social reformer ventured to interfere with marriage itself in the interests of eugenics, and sought to do what he could to obtain the kind of human material that he wanted, by breeding, before the time came for selection. The Spartan conscription, for the class that was subject to it (that is to say, for all free-born Spartiates who had not been exposed after birth), was universal. The Spartans took the children from their homes and put them into the educational mill at the age of seven. Finally, the Spartans not only conscripted and trained girls as well as boys, but they went far towards an identical treatment of both sexes. For Spartan girls, as well as for Spartan boys, conscription was universal; and the Spartan girls were not trained in special female accomplishments, nor kept in seclusion from the men. Spartan girls, like Spartan boys, were trained on a competitive system in athletics; and girls, like boys, competed naked in public before a male audience.

In the matter of breeding human stock, the Spartan system pursued two distinct aims simultaneously. It aimed both at quantity and at quality. It secured quantity (proportionately to the miniature scale on which the Spartan Society was built) by addressing itself to the individual male adult Spartiate and seeking to influence his behaviour through inducements and through penalties. The deliberate and confirmed bachelor was penalized by the State and was insulted by his juniors for his shameful lack of public spirit. On the other hand, the father of three sons was exempt from mobilization, and the father of four from all obligations towards the State. At the same time, quality was secured by keeping alive, with a conscious and definite eugenic purpose, certain primitive social customs governing sexual intercourse which appear to have been relics of a sex-group system of social organization antecedent to the system represented by marriage and the family. A Spartiate husband won popular approval, instead of exposing himself to public condemnation, if he took pains to improve the quality of his wife's progeny by arranging that her children should be gotten upon her by a sire who was a better man—or human animal—than her husband himself. And it even appears that a Spartiate wife could arrange this on her own account with impunity if her husband would not take the initiative in providing her with a substitute for himself when he was manifestly below par. The spirit in which the Spartans practised their eugenics is conveyed by Plutarch in a passage in which he says the Spartan social reformer

saw nothing but vulgarity and vanity in the sexual conventions of the rest of Mankind, who take care to serve their bitches and their mares with the best sires that they can manage to borrow or hire, yet lock their women up and keep them under watch and ward in order to make sure that they shall bear children exclusively to their husbands—as though this were a husband's sacred right even if he happens to be feebleminded or senile or diseased. This convention ignores the two obvious truths that bad parents produce bad childred and good parents good children, and that the first people to feel the difference will be those who possess the children and who have to bring them up.

In the matter of educating the Spartiate children which had been bred in this way, with the ultimate object of selecting the best of them for enrolment among the 'Peers' and endowment with public allotments, the Spartan system again availed itself of the relics of a pre-familial system of social organization in which the child who no longer needed his mother's personal care was educated, not by learning his father's business in a patriarchal household, but by successive membership in a series of 'human packs,' in which he consorted, at each stage, with the other children of the tribe who were of his own age and sex. The 'Lycurgean' reform adopted this 'age-class' system and at the same time adapted it to its own educational purpose by introducing a cross-division in which children of all ages were brought together in one group, so that the elder children might assist in training the younger. These juvenile 'droves' were reproductions of, and preparations for, the adult 'messes,' which were associations of 'Peers' belonging to different 'age-classes,' from the highest to the lowest, among the forty 'year-classes' (from the twenty-first to the sixtieth year inclusive) that were subject to military service. The climax of a Spartan boy's thirteen years of education in a 'drove' was his candidature, at the end of his twentieth year, for entry into one of the 'messes,' which was the sole avenue of admission into the fraternity of the 'Peers.' Entry into a 'mess' could only be secured by co-option; and a single 'black ball' entailed the rejection of the candidate. A successful candidate, once co-opted, remained an active member of his 'mess' for forty years unless he either failed to make his prescribed contribution, in victuals and money, towards the upkeep of the common table or were convicted of the unpardonable offence of cowardice in war.

The leading features in the Spartan system were: supervision, selection, and specialization; a competitive spirit; and the simultaneous use of the negative stimulus of punishment and the positive stimulus of reward. And in the Spartiate fraternity of 'Peers' these features were not confined to the educational stage. They continued to dominate the Spartiate's adult life as they had dominated his boyhood; and from the moment when he was taken away from his mother upon the completion of his seventh year he was continuously subject to discipline until the completion of his sixtieth year brought him his release from military service. The outward and visible sign of this discipline was the regulation which prescribed fifty-three years 'service with the colours'; for the Spartiate who had been transferred as a child from his parents' home to a juvenile 'drove' did not find himself at liberty to live in a home of his own when he had been co-opted into a 'mess' and had been endowed with a public allotment and had performed his social duty of taking a wife in marriage. The Spartiate 'Peers' were both compelled to marry and forbidden to lead a 'home life.' The Spartiate bridegroom was required to spend even his wedding-night in barracks; and, though the ban upon sleeping at home was gradually relaxed as he advanced in years, the ban upon dining at home was absolute and permanent.

Lycurgus took care that the Spartiates should not be at liberty to take a preliminary dinner at home and so come to mess on full stomachs. If a Spartiate showed no appetite at mess, he was 'told off' by his messmates as a glutton who was too soft to stand the common fare; and if he was actually convicted he was fined. There was a famous occasion when King Agis had returned from the wars after a long absence (at the end of his victorious war of attrition against Athens). The King wanted to dine, just once, with his wife, and sent to the mess for his portion; but the Army Council would not allow it to be sent, and, when the incident came to the notice of the Board of Overseers next day, they made the King pay a fine.[2]

Manifestly, a system which set 'human nature' at defiance so truculently as this could not have been enforced without some overwhelming external sanction; and at Sparta this sanc-

[2] Plutarch: *Apophthegmata Laconica: Lycurgus*, No. 6.

tion was applied by public opinion, which knew how to chas-
tise an offender against the Spartan social code with scorpions
that stung far more cruelly than the Overseers' whips. The
point is brought out by an Athenian observer [3] who studied
the Spartan system in its eleventh hour, on the eve of its collapse.

One of the remarkable achievements of Lycurgus is that he has
made it preferable, in Sparta, to die a noble death rather than remain alive in disgrace. As a matter of fact, investigation reveals that
there are actually fewer deaths in battle among the Spartans than
in armies which give way to fear and prefer to leave the field; so
that in reality courage turns out to be a more effective survival-
factor than cowardice. The path of courage is easier and more
agreeable and smoother and more secure . . . And I ought not to
omit to explain how Lycurgus made sure that this path should be
followed by his Spartans. He made sure of that by ensuring inevitable happiness for the brave and inevitable unhappiness for the
cowardly. In other communities, a coward's only penalty is to be
branded with the epithet. For the rest, he is free to work and play
cheek by jowl with men of valour if he chooses. In Sparta, on the
other hand, everybody would be ashamed to take a coward for his
messmate or to take him for his partner in athletics. And it will
often happen that when they are picking up ball-teams the coward
finds himself left out, and that in choirs he is pushed out into the
least honourable positions, and that he has to yield precedence to
everybody in the street and at table and to make way for his juniors and to keep his womenfolk indoors and to bear their re-
proaches for his lack of manhood and to resign himself to having
no housewife in his house and to pay a fine on that account into the
bargain, and never to show himself out of doors with his skin oiled,
and in fact to do nothing whatsoever that is done by Spartans who
have no stain on their reputations—under pain of receiving bodily
chastisement from his betters. For my part, I am not at all surprised
that, in a community in which cowardice is visited with this terrific penalization, death is preferable to a life of such reproach and
such dishonour.

[3] Xenophon: *Respublica Lacedaemoniorum*, ch. ix.

Yet penalization alone, however merciless, could never have created the Spartan êthos or have inspired the superhuman heroism which that êthos made possible. The sanction which made the Spartans what they were was internal as well as external; for these implacable souls, whose corporate public opinion made life intolerable for any one of their number who had failed to live up to their common standard of behaviour, were merciless in such cases just because they were single-hearted in exacting the same standard individually from themselves. This 'categorical imperative,' in the soul of every true Spartiate 'Peer,' was the ultimate driving force which made the 'Lycurgean' system work—in sheer defiance of 'human nature'—for more than two hundred years. And its essence is laid bare in the no doubt imaginary but none the less illuminating conversation which Herodotus puts into the mouths of the Achaemenian Pādishāh Xerxes and the exiled Spartan King Dâmarâtus, who was serving on Xerxes' staff, when Xerxes' army was marching upon Thermopylae from the Dardanelles. Xerxes has asked Dâmarâtus whether he is to expect any resistance; and Dâmarâtus has answered him that, whatever the other Hellenes may do, he can guarantee in regard to his own Spartan countrymen (though he personally has no cause to love them) that they will turn out to fight without taking any account of the disparity of numbers. When Xerxes refuses to entertain the idea that troops who are free agents, as the Spartans are *ex hypothesi*, would voluntarily face an ordeal into which Xerxes' own troops could only be driven by dread of their commander and by compulsion of the lash, Dâmarâtus replies that,

free though the Spartans are, they are not free altogether. They too serve a master in the shape of Law, whom they dread far more intensely than your servants dread you. They show this by doing whatever their master orders, and his orders are always the same:

'In action it is forbidden to retire in the face of enemy forces of whatever strength. Troops are to keep their formation and to conquer or die.'

This was the spirit that inspired the Spartans' achievements; and those achievements have stamped the Spartan name with the meaning which it still bears in every living language to-day. The deeds are so famous that there is no need in this place to retell familiar tales. The story of Leonidas and the Three Hundred at Thermopylae: is it not written in the Seventh Book of Herodotus? And the story of the Boy and the Fox: is it not written in Plutarch's *Life of Lycurgus?* And do not these two stories, between them, convey the whole *tour de force* of Spartan boyhood and Spartan manhood? And if we cannot take our eyes off the Spartans—as, in candour, we cannot—without first looking also at the other side of the Spartan shield, we have simply to remind ourselves that the last two years of a Spartan boy's education before his coming of age—the crucial years upon which, more than any others, his prospects of co-option on to a 'mess' depended—were probably spent in the Secret Service, and that this was nothing else than an official 'murder gang' which patrolled the Laconian countryside surreptitiously—taking cover by day and stalking abroad, like a veritable *negotium perambulans in tenebris,* by night—for the purpose of making away with any Helots who had shown symptoms of restiveness or perhaps merely vestiges of character and ability. While Sparta demanded, and duly evoked, the manly heroism of a Leonidas and his Three Hundred in order to cover the Spartan name with incomparable military glory, she equally demanded—and did not fail to evoke—the juvenile criminality of her Secret Service in order that the tiny minority of Spartiate 'Peers' might keep their feet on the necks of a numerically overwhelming majority of 'Inferiors' and 'Dependants' and 'New Members' and 'Serfs' who would have

been delighted, if ever they had the chance, 'to eat' their hand-
ful of masters 'alive.' If, under the 'Lycurgean' system, the
Spartans rose to some of the sublimest heights of human conduct, they also sounded some of the darkest depths.

Every feature in the 'Lycurgean' system—material or spiritual, evil or good—was directed towards one single aim; and
this definite aim was exactly achieved. Under the 'Lycurgean'
system, the Lacedaemonian heavy infantry were the best heavy
infantry in the Hellenic World. They were far superior to any
other Hellenic troops of the same arm. For nearly two centuries the armies of other Hellenic Powers dreaded to meet
the Lacedaemonian Army in pitched battle. In drill and in
morale alike, the Lacedaemonians were inimitable. But, just because of this, there was no room, in 'Lycurgean' Sparta, for
more than one kind of professionalism.

The 'single-track' genius of the 'Lycurgean' *agôgê* leaps to
the eye of any visitor to the present-day Sparta Museum. For
this museum is totally unlike any other modern collection of
extant Hellenic works of art, either in Greece or elsewhere.
In other such collections the visitor's eye seeks out and finds
and dwells upon the works of 'the Classical Age,' which approximately coincides with the fifth and fourth centuries B.C.
In the Sparta Museum, however, this 'Classical' Hellenic art is
conspicuous by its absence. The visitor's eye is here caught
first, and fascinated, by the 'pre-classical' exhibits: delicate
ivory-carving and striking polychrome pottery painted by
artists who had a gift for line as well as colour. Fragmentary
though they are, these relics of early Spartan art bear unmis-
takable marks of originality and individuality; and the visitor
who has made the discovery of them here for the first time
looks expectantly to find the sequel—only to look in vain, since
this early blossoming of Spartan art remains a promise without
a fulfilment. In the place which should contain the monuments

of a Spartan version of 'Classical' art there is a great hiatus; and the Sparta Museum contains little more except a superfluity of uninspired and standardized works of minor sculpture dating from the late Hellenistic and early Imperial period. Between the two sets of exhibits in the Sparta Museum a great chronological gulf is fixed; and this gulf is explained by the dates. The date at which the early Spartan art breaks off is approximately that of the Overseership of Chilon in the middle of the sixth century B.C. The almost equally abrupt resumption of 'artistic production' in the age of decadence is posterior to 189–188 B.C.: the date at which the 'Lycurgean' system is known to have been abolished at Sparta by the deliberate policy of a foreign conqueror after Sparta had been forcibly incorporated into the Achaean League. Art was impossible at Sparta so long as Spartan life was confined, by this cast-iron system, to the single track of militarism.

The paralysis which descended, with the *agôgê*, upon Spartan pictorial and glyptic art was equally fatal to the art of music, in which the Spartans had likewise shown early promise. The Spartan authorities even discouraged their nationals from cultivating an art which is so near akin to the soldier's that, in our modern Western World, it is regarded as the best preparation for a military training. The Spartans were prohibited from competing in the great Pan-Hellenic athletic sports, on the ground that professionalism in running and jumping and putting the weight was one thing and professionalism in wielding the spear and the shield and performing the evolutions of the parade-ground was something quite different, from which the Spartiate's heart and mind must not be distracted on any account.

Thus Sparta paid the penalty for having taken her own headstrong and hazardous course at the parting of the ways in the eighth century B.C. by condemning herself, in the sixth century, to standing still—with arms presented like a soldier on parade—at a moment when other Hellenes were just moving forward once again on one of the most signal moves in the whole course of Hellenic history.

It requires an effort of imagination to remind ourselves that the fraternity of Spartiate 'Peers' was the earliest Hellenic democracy, and that the redivision of the arable land of Messenia among the members of this Spartiate dêmos in equal allotments became the watchword of the revolution that convulsed Athens in the next generation. In Sparta the new movement which had declared itself precociously in the 'Lycurgean' reform was doomed to be arrested prematurely at a rudimentary stage because the 'Lycurgean' system changed the face of Spartan life, only to petrify it for ever after. It was not in Sparta, and not in response to the peculiar challenge that had been presented to the Spartans in the Second Messeno-Spartan War, that these new tendencies in Hellenic life were destined to work themselves out in fresh acts of creation. The creative act of the sixth century B.C. was evoked by a challenge of a different kind; and this challenge was presented in the first instance to those Hellenic communities which had responded to the previous challenge of the eighth century, not on the Spartan lines of conquering a next-door neighbour in Hellas, but on the Chalcidian and Megarian lines of overseas colonization.

After the Malthusian problem had been solved—or shelved—in Hellas at large by this method for a period of some two centuries, it was raised again, and this time more acutely than before, by the simultaneous stoppage of the territorial expansion of the Hellenic World in every quarter. Eastward, Hellenic expansion was checked in the sixth century B.C. by the rise of new Great Powers—the Saïte Power in Egypt and the Lydian in Anatolia and the far mightier Achaemenian Empire that first overshadowed and then absorbed them both. During the same century, Hellenic expansion was brought to a halt in the Western Mediterranean by a rally among the rival Levantine colonial peoples—Phoenicians and Etruscans—who now discovered in political co-operation a make-weight for their inferiority to the Greeks in vitality and numbers. At the same time the indigenous barbarians of the West were beginning to learn how to hold their own against all the Levantine intruders alike by fighting them with their own weapons. In these various ways the expansion of Hellas was cut short all round; and this challenge stimulated the Hellenes to solve their recurrent social problem by substituting, for the mere extensive growth which was no longer open to them, an intensive growth, of a higher social order, which was still within their capacity. They passed from 'subsistence farming' to 'cash-crop farming' and manufactures; from a régime of local self-sufficiency to a régime of international trade; from a natural economy to a money economy; and from a polity based on birth to a polity based on property. And the lead in making this victorious response was taken by Athens: a 'dark horse' who had not taken part in the earlier movement of overseas colonization, but who at the same time had not followed Sparta into her Messenian blind-alley.

The nature of the Athenian response has only to be mentioned in order to point the contrast between Hellenic progress under Athenian leadership and Sparta's un-Hellenic immobility; and this contrast is aptly symbolized in the difference between the Attic and the Spartan money-coinage. The new invention of coined money had found its way into Sparta before the 'Lycurgean' system set hard; and even thereafter it continued to play a not unimportant part in the internal life of the fraternity of Spartiate 'Peers,' since a 'Peer's' contribution to his 'mess,' which he had to keep up under pain of forfeiting his membership, was payable partly in money as well as in kind. Yet although the sixth-century Spartan reformers could not, or would not, banish coin from Laconia altogether, they succeeded in adapting this institution to their purpose like all the other institutions which they found in the field. They allowed their countrymen to retain a token-currency of iron which was too heavy and bulky for ordinary convenience and was chemically treated in such a way as to make it too poor in quality to have any intrinsic commercial value even in bulk. Thus Laconia was excluded from the international continuum of financial relations, just as effectively as if she had possessed no coinage at all, by being given a coinage which could have no currency beyond the Laconian frontiers. Meanwhile 'the owls of Athene' became the current coin of the entire Mediterranean World, and the occasional arrival of a flock of these migratory birds in Sparta itself created still greater consternation among the Spartan authorities than the importation of a musical instrument with more than seven strings. The Spartiate Gylippus himself, who had done perhaps as much as any other single man to bring Athens to the ground in the Great War of 431–404 B.C. by foiling the Athenian attempt to conquer Sicily, was forced to go into exile on the morrow of the peace when his servant laid information that there was 'a bevy of owls in the tilery.'

Thus the 'Lycurgean' system, which the Spartans established in order to defend their dominion over the Helots at home, had the effect of throwing them on the defensive against the whole Hellenic World into the bargain. And the greatest irony in Sparta's situation was the fact that, when she had sacrificed everything that made life worth living to the single object of forging an irresistible military instrument, she found that she dared not make use of her dearly bought power because her social equilibrium under the 'Lycurgean' system was so exact, and her social tension so high, that the slightest disturbance of the *status quo* might have disastrous repercussions; and this disaster might be brought on by a victory which would increase the permanent demands on Sparta's man-power almost as readily as by a defeat which would open the way for an invasion of Sparta's home-territories. In the event, the fatal victory of 404 B.C. and the consequent fatal defeat of the year 371 duly brought upon the Spartans the disaster which they had never ceased to dread since they had succeeded in making themselves into the most formidable military power in their world. Yet Spartan statesmanship managed to postpone the evil day for nearly two centuries, dating from the completion of the 'Lycurgean' reforms, by declining to accept for Sparta the greatness which circumstances incessantly sought to thrust upon her.

In this frame of mind the Spartans evaded, time and again, the challenge to assume the leadership of Hellas which the Achaemenian peril presented to them. They forbore to send help to the Anatolian Greek insurgents in 499 B.C.; they arrived too late to fight at Marathon in 490; and, after covering themselves with glory, under protest, at Thermopylae and Plataea, they abdicated from the high command of the forces of liberation in 479–478. Rather than incur the risks which greatness involved for Sparta, they deliberately left their own repudiated greatness lying derelict for Athens to appropriate; and yet, even at this bitter price, they were ultimately unable to elude their tragic destiny. For the Spartans' great refusal to accept the challenge of 499–479 B.C. did not, and could not, purchase for Sparta more than a brief immunity from her peculiar dilemma. In preferring, to the risks of acceptance, the lesser immediate evil of giving the Athenians their opportunity, the Spartans were opening the door for the menace to Hellenic liberties to recur in the shape of an Athenian peril; and this time the Spartans found themselves confronted with a chal-

lenge which it was impossible for them to ignore. In the opinion of Thucydides, 'the fundamental . . . cause of the Atheno-
Peloponnesian War was the fear inspired in the Lacedaemonians by the rise of Athens to greatness; and this fear compelled
them to take up arms'—under threat of seeing the 'sanitary
cordon' of their Peloponnesian alliance dissolve and their Athenian enemy from beyond the Isthmus join hands, to their undoing, with their Messenian enemy within their gates.

In 431 B.C. Corinthian diplomacy succeeded in compelling
Spartan statesmanship to assume the leadership of Hellas at
last; and, in the Great War of 431–404, the Spartan military
machine—now tested for the first time to the uttermost—performed all that its makers had intended, and all that Sparta's
neighbours hoped or feared. The Spartan nightmare of an
union sacrée between Athens and the Helots did not come
true—not even when the Athenian strategist Demosthenes made
his brilliant stroke of establishing a fortified post at Pylos, on
the Messenian coast of Laconia, in 425 B.C. On the other hand,
the overland expedition of the Spartan commander Brasidas
to the Thracian seaboard, and the exhaustion of Athenian
strength in Nicias' naval expedition to Sicily, did bring to pass
the Athenian nightmare that the Peloponnesians might succeed
in joining hands with the Hellenic subjects of Athens on the
other side of the Aegean, and might overpower Athens on her
own element with a fleet manned by Ionian seamen and fi-
nanced by Achaemenian gold. When this first stage in the
self-inflicted attrition of the Hellenic Society came to an end
in the year 404 B.C., it was Athens and not Sparta that lay prostrate. Yet the Spartan King Agis' prophecy—uttered at the
moment when the die was cast—that 'this day' would prove to
'be the beginning of great evils for Hellas' came true in respect of the victors no less than the vanquished; for the greatness which Sparta now tardily and involuntarily retrieved from

her prostrated rival proved to be a veritable Shirt of Nessus.

The Spartans were placed in a peculiar predicament by their victorious war of 431–404 B.C. A people trained consummately but exclusively for warlike contact with their neighbours found themselves suddenly compelled, by the outcome of one particular war, to enter into non-military relations for which they were not only unprepared but were positively unfitted by their own peculiar institutions and habits and êthos. These peculiarities which the Spartans had developed in order to grapple with a previous problem, and which had given them superhuman strength within the limits of the narrow environment within which their lines had previously been cast, now took their revenge upon this peculiar people by making them inhumanly or infra-humanly incompetent to live in the wider world into which the fortunes of war had eventually carried them. The very exactness of their adaptation to their previous environment made any readaptation to a new environment so difficult for them as to be virtually impossible; and the very qualities which had been the secret of their success in the one situation became their worst enemies when they found themselves in the other. The Spartans came to grief when, in consequence of a military victory, they had to take upon their own shoulders the imperial responsibilities of Athens instead of merely holding the naval and military power of Athens at bay.

The contrast between the Spartan at home and the Spartan abroad was a by-word in Hellas; for whereas, on his own ground, the Spartan admittedly rose above the ordinary Hellenic standards of personal discipline and disinterestedness, he fell below those same standards in at least equal measure as soon as he found himself out of his own element. The spectacular demoralization of the Spartan Regent Pausanias, when circumstances placed him in command of a Pan-Hellenic force on Achaemenian territory, had been an awful warning which

had counted for much in the Spartan Government's decision
to abdicate from the leadership of Hellas in 479–478 B.C. And
this decision was almost justified in retrospect when, in and
after the second and conclusive round of the Great War of
431–404 B.C., Sparta was forced to send abroad Pausaniases by
the dozen. 'We have done those things which we ought not
to have done and we have left undone those things which we
ought to have done, and there is no health in us' must have
been the reflection that forced itself, on the morrow of Leuctra,
upon the mind of a Spartan statesman like King Agesilaus who
was old enough to remember the *ancien régime*.

In that year 371 B.C. the majority of the Spartiate 'Peers'
were serving, outside the frontiers of Laconia, on garrison duty
in other Hellenic states which had once been Sparta's voluntary allies, but which could no longer be held to their allegiance except by naked military force; and the pick of them
had been seconded from their military duties in order to occupy political and administrative posts in which they were
making themselves as notorious, on a petty scale, as Pausanias
himself, for their Spartan tactlessness and tyranny and corruption, until the respectable title of 'moderators,' by which these
Spartan martinets abroad were called, had come to sound
odious in Hellenic ears. These very Spartiate 'Peers,' who were
making the Spartan name stink as foully as fish out of water,
would no doubt have manifested the traditional Spartan virtues
if Fate had allowed them to fulfil the expectations in which
they had grown up by leaving them to live their camp-life on
the banks of the Eurotas until the Lacedaemonian Army was
mobilized for the Leuctra campaign. Unfortunately for their
own reputation and their country's, all these men were absent
at that grave hour, and, in the Lacedaemonian contingent of
the army under King Cleombrotus' command which was so
signally defeated by the Thebans at Leuctra in 371 B.C., there

were only 400 Spartiates in action apart from the 300 'knights'
who always formed a Spartan King's personal bodyguard on
active service. This figure seems to mean that, in the Lacedaemonian infantry of the line, on this critical occasion, only one
man was a Spartiate in every ten, instead of the four Spartiates
in every ten Lacedaemonians which was the regulation quota.
If the Spartiate quota had not been thus cut down, at Leuctra,
to a quarter of its normal strength, we may doubt whether
even the valour of the Theban infantrymen and the tactical
genius of the Theban commander Epaminondas, who knew
how to turn his troops' fighting-power to the best account,
would have been able to achieve their historic success of breaking that record of Lacedaemonian invincibility which had remained unbroken, down to that date, for at least two centuries
and a half.

Moreover, the Spartan victory over Athens in the Great
War of 431–404 B.C. ruined Sparta in other and subtler ways,
besides the compulsion which it put upon her to second her
'Peers' from military service, from which they could not safely
be spared, to non-military duties with which they could not
safely be entrusted. It ruined her, for example, by exposing her
belatedly, and therefore disastrously, to the subversive social effects of a money economy from which her people had so long
been artificially sheltered. 'The date at which Lacedaemon was
first attacked by social disease and corruption practically coincides with the moment at which she overthrew the Athenian
Empire and gorged herself with the precious metals.' [4] And the
introduction of a money economy brought in its train an
equally subversive revolution in the Spartan attitude towards
personal property. Spartan conservatism could not, indeed,
bring itself to go the length of allowing real estate to be bought
and sold in the market; but at some date unknown in the

[4] Plutarch's *Life of Agis*, ch. v.

fourth century B.C. the Spartan Assembly passed into law 'a bill making it legal for the holder of a family property or an allotment to give it away during his lifetime, or to bequeath it by will, to anybody whom he chose.' [5] The effect of this piece of legislation in reducing the numbers of the Spartiate 'Peers' must have been much greater than the effect of the relatively light Spartiate casualties at Leuctra, and possibly as great as the effect of the loss of Messenia, which was the political penalty of Sparta's military defeat. When Aristotle was writing his *Politics*, this unfortunate law was already producing noticeably untoward results. By the time of King Agis the Martyr, who came to the throne early in the latter half of the third century B.C., 'not more than 700 Spartiates survived, and of these perhaps 100 may have owned land and an allotment, while the remainder were a destitute and disfranchised mob.' [6]

Another conspicuous social phenomenon in the Spartan decadence was 'the monstrous regiment of women.' Like the maldistribution of property, this maldistribution of influence and authority as between the two sexes was already noticeable at Sparta in Aristotle's time; and in the legend of the Saviour Kings, Agis and Cleomenes, who reigned at Sparta a century later, the part assigned to the noble women who inspire and encourage and console and mourn the heroes is as prominent as it is in the New Testament. This legend suggests that, notwithstanding Aristotle's strictures on the behaviour of the Spartan women during Epaminondas' invasion of the Eurotas Valley in the winter of 370–369 B.C., it was really through their virtues that, in the age of Spartan decadence, the Spartan women established their moral ascendancy over their husbands and their sons; and, if this is the truth, it throws some light upon the failure of the 'Lycurgean' system. For, although the

---

[5] Plutarch's *Life of Agis*, ch. v.
[6] Plutarch's *Life of Agis*, ch. v.

system had been applied to women as well as to men, the Spartan girls and Spartan married women had not been subjected to its pressure in the same degree as their brothers and their husbands; and if we are right in our belief that the moral breakdown of Spartan manhood was the penalty of a moral rigidity which had been produced by the excessive severity of the 'Lycurgean' temper, then we may conjecture that it was the relative immunity of the women from this unnatural strain that left them with the moral elasticity to bend and rebound in reaction to an ordeal which broke the spirit of the Spartan men outright.

The epitaph of the 'Lycurgean' system has been written by Aristotle in the form of a general proposition:

Peoples ought not to train themselves in the art of war with an eye to subjugating neighbours who do not deserve to be subjugated . . . The paramount aim of any social system should be to frame military institutions, like all its other institutions, with an eye to the circumstances of peace-time, when the soldier is off duty; and this proposition is borne out by the facts of experience. For militaristic states are apt to survive only so long as they remain at war, while they go to ruin as soon as they have finished making their conquests. Peace causes their metal to lose its temper; and the fault lies with a social system which does not teach its soldiers what to make of their lives when they are off duty.

Thus the 'Lycurgean' system ultimately and inevitably destroyed itself; yet, even in committing suicide, the system died hard. Although it had been brought into existence for the precise purpose of enabling Sparta to maintain possession of Messenia, the 'Lycurgean' *agôgê* actually continued to be practised at Sparta, out of sheer conservatism, for nearly two centuries after Messenia had been irrevocably lost. And, although King Cleomenes the Martyr tardily replaced the 4,000 lost Spartiate allotments in Messenia by redividing the territory that remained to Sparta east of Taygetus, in the Eurotas Valley, into new allotments of an equal number, the royal revolutionary did not take this opportunity to liberate his country from the ancient curse of helotage. Since the 700 surviving Spartiates, all told, could not take up as much as 20 per cent. of the 4,000 allotments into which the estates of the 100 surviving Spartiate 'Peers' were now broken up, Cleomenes presumably gave the Spartan franchise to more than 3,000 Helots and Perioeci in order to fill up the numbers of his new Spartan citizen-body; but these were only a minority of the surviving Helots; for Cleomenes freed 6,000 more of them, at so much a head in ready money, and enrolled 2,000 of these freedmen in his army, on the eve of the Battle of Sellasia, when his Macedonian adversary Antigonus Dôsôn had reached Tegea. And when the Romans invaded Laconia in 195 B.C., they found Helots still living on there in their traditional status.

The most remarkable feat of Spartan 'Diehardism' was the attempt of the Royal Martyrs, Agis and Cleomenes, to reclothe the dry bones of the 'Lycurgean' system in flesh, and to breathe the breath of new life into the corpse, a full century and a half after the great Spartan victory over Athens had sealed the 'Lycurgean' system's fate. In this last desperate *tour de force* the derelict wheel of Spartan life was turned, by a supreme conservative effort, so very far back that it actually made a revolution; and this violent movement finally wrecked the long-dislocated mechanism. Cleomenes' surgery effectively killed a body social which it could not possibly cure. The bruised reed was broken by the hand that sought to straighten it; and the smoking flax was quenched for ever by the breath which was intended to rekindle a flame.

Thereafter Sparta lived wholly in her dreams of the past and distinguished herself—if it be a distinction—in nothing but the peculiar zest with which she threw herself into the academic game of archaism that was in fashion throughout the Hellenic World during the first two centuries of the Roman Empire. The Spartans of the Imperial age delighted, like all their contemporaries, in composing honorary inscriptions in a caricature of their obsolete local dialect; but at Sparta these harmless archaistic pedantries were accompanied by at least one archaistic morbidity of a gruesome nature. A primitive fertility-rite of scourging boys at the altar of Artemis Orthia, which had been converted by the 'Lycurgean' system, for its own grim but still utilitarian purposes, into a competition in the endurance of pain, was exaggerated, in Plutarch's day, into a sadistic atrocity, in which boys were keyed up to a pitch of hysteria at which they submitted to be flogged to death. 'This would not be incredible of the Spartan youth of the present day,' Plutarch writes in recounting the famous legendary story of the Spartan boy and the stolen fox, 'since I myself have seen numbers of them die under the flogging at Orthia's altar.' The essence of this scene, in which a superhuman—or inhuman —feat of endurance is performed without flinching, yet to no effect, is characteristic of the Spartan êthos and emblematic of Sparta's fate. For if any Spartiate ever prayed, for the peace of his soul, that *tantus labor non sit cassus*, that prayer was assuredly breathed by Spartan lips in vain.

The vanity of Spartan wishes is exposed in the outcome of an otherwise unimportant arbitral transaction which the Roman historian Tacitus records—apparently without realizing its historic significance—in his annals of the Roman Empire in the year 25 of the Christian Era:

A hearing was given to delegations from the Lacedaemonian and Messenian Governments in the matter of the juridical status of the temple of Diana [i.e. Artemis] Limnâtis. The Lacedaemonians maintained that the temple had been founded by their own Lacedaemonian forefathers on Lacedaemonian territory, and they supported their claim by an appeal to literary evidence, both historical and poetic. They declared that the temple had been taken from them forcibly in war, by Philip of Macedon, and had afterwards been restored to them on the strength of a legal opinion which had been rendered by Gaius Caesar and Marcus Antonius. The Messenians, on their side, brought up the ancient division of the Peloponnese among the descendants of Hercules [i.e. Hêraklês], and maintained that the territory of Dentheliâtis, in which the temple was situated, had been part of the portion assigned to their king. They declared that there were actual records of the transaction still extant, engraved on stone and on archaic bronze; and they added that, if there was to be an appeal to literary evidence, they could also beat the Lacedaemonians in the amount and in the fulness of the testimony of this kind which they were in a position to cite. As for King Philip's decision, they argued that it had not been an act of arbitrary power, but had been based upon the facts and had been confirmed by identic judgements of the Macedonian king Antigonus and the Roman general Mummius; by an arbitral decision of the Milesian Government; and most recently by the decision of Atidius Geminus, the Governor of the Roman Province of Achaia. On this showing, judgement was now given in the Messenian Government's favour.

Thus, in the first century of the Christian Era, the Spartans were still contending—and this last time without success—over the debatable territory in the mountainous borderland between the Eurotas Valley and Messenia which their forefathers had originally contended for, and conquered, in the eighth century B.C. A dispute over the Dentheliâtis was the traditional cause of the First Messeno-Spartan War; and now, after the passage of at least eight centuries, the same dispute between the same two parties over the same insignificant piece of territory was at issue before the arbitral tribunal of the Roman Emperor Tiberius. Assuredly no further proof is needed that the Spartans were veritably a people without a history.

CHAPTER IV

Assyria, the Strong Man Armed

———

The blindness of the militarist is the theme of a famous parable in the New Testament:

> When a strong man armed keepeth his palace, his goods are in peace; but when a stronger than he shall come upon him and overcome him, he taketh from him all his armour wherein he trusted, and divideth his spoils.

The militarist is so confident of his own ability to look after himself in that social—or anti-social—system in which all disputes are settled *manu militari*, and not by process of law or conciliation, that he throws his sword into the scales when the issue between a régime of violence and a régime of organized peace is trembling in the balance. The sword's weight duly tips the balance in favour of the continuance of the old barbaric dispensation; and the militarist, exultant at having once more made his will prevail, now points to this latest triumph as a final proof that the sword is omnipotent. In the next chapter of the story, however, it turns out that he has failed to prove his thesis *ad hominem* in the particular case which exclusively interests him; for the next event is his own overthrow by a stronger militarist than himself. His success in prolonging the militarist régime has simply insured that he himself shall learn, at last, what it feels like to have one's throat

cut. We may think of the Aztecs and the Incas, each remorse-
lessly warring down their weaker neighbours in their own respective worlds, until they are overtaken by Spanish *conquistadores* who fall upon them from another world and strike
them down with weapons for which theirs are no match. It is
equally illuminating, and considerably more profitable, to think
of ourselves.

In the Hellenic Mythology the doom which 'the strong man
armed' invincibly insists upon bringing upon himself is portrayed in the legend of how Cronos brutally supplants his
father Uranus in the lordship of the Universe, only to taste,
in his turn, of Uranus' experience at the hands of the usurper's
own son Zeus. In Zeus we have the picture of the militarist
who is saved in spite of himself, thanks to the suffering of another being who is nobler, as well as wiser, than he is; and
Prometheus' salvation of Zeus is a Hellenic counterpart of
Jesus' salvation of Peter when Peter commits the militarist's
crime at the crucial moment in the Garden of Gethsemane.

And, behold, one of them which were with Jesus stretched
out his hand and drew his sword and struck a servant of the High
Priest's and smote off his ear. Then said Jesus unto him: 'Put up
again thy sword into his place; for all they that take the sword
shall perish with the sword.'

In the Old Testament the classic portrayal of the militarist's
self-contrived discomfiture is given in the story of Ben-Hadad
and Ahab. When King Ben-Hadad of Damascus is besieging
King Ahab of Israel in his city of Samaria, the aggressor sends
messengers into the beleaguered city to demand of his victim
the surrender of everything that he possesses, and Ahab returns
the soft answer: 'My lord, O king, according to thy saying,
I am thine and all that I have.' But Ben-Hadad will not forbear
from humiliating his humble adversary still further; so he

sends a second message to inform Ahab that the conqueror's
servants will now come to search his house, and that, 'whatsoever is pleasant in' Ahab's 'eyes, they shall put it in their hand
and take it away.' Thereupon Ahab replies that he still accepts
the first demand but rejects the second; and, when Ben-Hadad
proceeds to breathe fire and slaughter, Ahab says to the bearers
of this third message: 'Tell him: "Let not him that girdeth on
his harness boast himself as he that putteth it off." ' Thereafter,
according to Ben-Hadad's will and against the wishes of Ahab,
the issue between the two kings is decided in a pitched battle;
and in this battle the aggressor brings upon himself an overwhelming defeat. The story ends with a tableau in which the
servants of Ben-Hadad come out—from the city in which they
and their master are now being besieged in their turn—with
sackcloth on their loins and ropes on their heads, and plead
with the victorious Ahab for mercy. And Ahab is not betrayed
into making Ben-Hadad's mistake by the 'reversal of roles' that
has so swiftly inverted the two kings' respective positions. To
the message 'Thy servant Ben-Hadad saith: "I pray thee, let
me live," ' Ahab answers: 'Is he yet alive? He is my brother.'
And, when, on his instructions, Ben-Hadad is brought with
honour into his presence, Ahab makes a treaty with his peni-
tent opponent—on the extremely favourable terms which Ben-
Hadad is in haste to offer him—and then straightway lets him
go free.

We may next consider the case of the Assyrian militarism
which cast its shadow over the Syriac World in Ahab's and
Ben-Hadad's generation.

The disaster in which the Assyrian military power met its
end in 614–610 B.C. was even more overwhelming than those
which overtook the Macedonian phalanx in 197 and 168 B.C. or
the Roman legions in 53 B.C. and A.D. 378 or the Egyptian
Mamlūks in A.D. 1516–17 and A.D. 1798. The disaster at Pydna

cost Macedon her political independence; the disaster at Adrianople was surmounted by the Roman Empire at the price of 'scrapping' the defeated legionary and enlisting the victorious cataphract in his place; the French repetition of the original Ottoman blow was needed in order to remove the Mamlūk incubus, once for all, from the backs of an Egyptian peasantry which managed to survive the French and the Ottoman as well as the Mamlūk domination. On the other hand the disaster which was the end of the Assyrian military power capped the destruction of the Assyrian war-machine with the extinction of the Assyrian state and the extermination of the Assyrian people. In 614–610 B.C. a community which had been in existence for more than two thousand years, and had been playing an ever more dominant part in South-Western Asia over a period of some two and a half centuries, was blotted out almost completely.

The noise of a whip and the noise of the rattling of the wheels and of the prancing horses and of the jumping chariots.

The horseman lifteth up both the bright sword and the glittering spear; and there is a multitude of slain and a great number of carcases; and there is none end of their corpses—they stumble upon their corpses . . .

Thy shepherds slumber, O King of Assyria; thy nobles shall dwell in the dust; thy people is scattered upon the mountains, and no man gathereth them.

In this instance the curse of the victim who had lived to see his oppressor's fall was fulfilled in the sequel with an extraordinary precision. In 401 B.C., when Cyrus the Younger's ten thousand Greek mercenaries were retreating up the Tigris Valley from the battle-field of Cunaxa towards the Black Sea coast, they passed in succession the sites of Calah and Nineveh, and were struck with astonishment, not so much at the mas-

siveness of the fortifications and the extent of the area which
they embraced, as at the spectacle of such vast works of Man
lying uninhabited. The weirdness of these empty shells, which
testified by their inanimate endurance to the vigour of a vanished life, is vividly conveyed by the literary art of a member
of the Greek expeditionary force who has recounted its ex-
periences. Yet what is still more astonishing to a modern Western reader of Xenophon's narrative—acquainted, as he is, with
the history of Assyria, thanks to the achievements of our modern Western archaeologists—is to find that, although Xenophon's imagination was deeply struck, and his curiosity keenly
aroused, by the mystery of these deserted cities, he was unable
to learn even the most elementary facts about their authentic
history. Although the whole of South-Western Asia, from
Jerusalem to Ararat and from Elam to Lydia, had been dominated and terrorized by the masters of these cities at a Time-
distance of little more than two centuries from the date at
which Xenophon passed that way, the best account that he is
able to give of them—presumably on the authority of the
Greek army's local guides—is more wildly fabulous than the
account of the Egyptian Pyramid-Builders which has found
its way into the work of Herodotus after having travelled in
the solvent waters of the stream of 'folk-memory' for the
length of little less than two and a half millennia. As Xenophon
heard the story of Calah and Nineveh, these were two cities
of the Medes which had been besieged by the Persians when
Cyrus was wresting the empire from Astyages, and had been
miraculously depopulated by divine intervention after the Persians had found themselves unable to take them by storm. Not
even the bare name of Assyria was associated with the sites of
her second and third capitals in the current legends, attaching
to these sites, which came to the ears of the passing Greek
inquirer.

Where is the dwelling of the lions and the feedingplace of the young lions, where the lion, even the old lion, walked, and the lion's whelp, and none made them afraid?

As a matter of fact, if the Ten Thousand had happened to march up the right bank of the Tigris, instead of crossing, as they did, to the left bank at Sittace on the Babylon-Susa road, they would have passed the site of Asshur—the first and eponymous capital of the *Assyrium nomen*—and here they would have found, still squatting among the ruins, a small and miserable population that had not forgotten its historical title to the Assyrian name. Yet Xenophon's fabulous account of Calah and Nineveh is nearer to 'the philosophic truth' than our own archaeologists' discovery of the traces left by the squatters at Asshur; for in substance the catastrophe of 614–610 B.C. did wipe Assyria out; and in the Achaemenian Empire of Xenophon's day the surviving Assyrian helots were incomparably less conspicuous than the vestiges of the peoples round about, whom the Assyrian militarists had once trampled under foot and ground, as they thought, to powder. In an age when the very name and nationality of Nineveh or Calah were forgotten, Susa, which had been sacked by Asshurbanipal's army *circa* 639 B.C., was the capital of an empire whose effective dominion now extended, in almost every direction, an immense distance beyond the farthest points ever reached by Assyrian raiders. One of the subsidiary capitals of this empire was Babylon, which had been sacked by Sennacherib in 689 B.C. The Phoenician city-states, which the Assyrians had incessantly bullied and fleeced from the ninth century to the seventh, were now autonomous and contented members of a Syriac universal state; and even the Syriac and Hittite communities of the interior, which had apparently been pounded into pulp by the Assyrian flail, had contrived to retain a semblance of their former statehood in the guise of hierocratically administered temple-states.

In fact, within two centuries of Assyria's fall it had become clear that the Assyrian militarists had done their work for the benefit of others, and for the greatest benefit of those whom they had used the most despitefully. In grinding down the highland peoples of the Zagros and the Taurus the Assyrians had opened a passage for the Cimmerian and Scythian Nomads to make their descent upon the Babylonic and Syriac worlds; in deporting the broken peoples of Syria to the opposite extremity of their empire they had placed the Syriac Society in a position to encircle and eventually assimilate the Babylonic Society to which the Assyrians themselves belonged; in imposing a political unity upon the heart of South-Western Asia by main force they had prepared the ground for their own 'successor-states'—Media, Babylonia, Egypt, and Lydia—and for these successors' common heir, the Achaemenian Empire. Why was it that in the sequel to the long Assyrian terror the monster came off, as these comparisons and contrasts show, so very much worse than his victims?

The victims themselves, in retrospect, could only explain this tremendous 'reversal of roles' by invoking 'the Envy of the Gods.'

Behold, the Assyrian was a cedar in Lebanon with fair branches and with a shadowing shroud and of an high stature; and his top was among the thick boughs . . .

The cedars in the garden of God could not hide him; the fir trees were not like his boughs, and the chestnut trees were not like his branches; nor any tree in the Garden of God was like unto him in his beauty.

I have made him fair by the multitude of his branches, so that all the trees of Eden, that were in the Garden of God, envied him.

Therefore thus saith the Lord God: 'Because thou hast lifted up thyself in height, and he hath shot up his top among the thick boughs, and his heart is lifted up in his height—

'I have therefore delivered him into the hand of the mighty

one of the heathen; he shall surely deal with him; I have driven him out for his wickedness.

'And strangers, the terrible of the nations, have cut him off and have left him; upon the mountains and in all the valleys his branches are fallen; and his boughs are broken by all the rivers of the land; and all the people of the Earth are gone down from his shadow and have left him.'

Are we able in this instance to interpret the working of 'the Envy of the Gods' in terms of the stricken creature's own behaviour? At first sight the fate of Assyria does, indeed, seem difficult to comprehend; for her militarists cannot be convicted of the passive aberration to which we may attribute the undoing of the Macedonians and the Romans and the Mamlūks, who 'rested on their oars.' At the time when the Mamlūk and Roman and Macedonian war-machines each met with its fatal accident they were each of them long since static, hopelessly obsolete, and shockingly out of repair. On the other hand the Assyrian war-machine, which is singled out by the completeness of its final disaster, is also distinguished from these other war-machines—in what would seem to be the opposite sense— by the efficiency with which it was being perpetually overhauled and renovated and reinforced right down to the day of its destruction. The fund of military genius which produced the embryo of the hoplite in the fourteenth century B.C., on the eve of Assyria's first bid for predominance in South-Western Asia, and the embryo of the cataphract horse-archer in the seventh century B.C., on the eve of Assyria's own annihilation, was also productive throughout the seven intervening centuries, and never more so than in the final paroxysm of the four historic bouts in which the Assyrian militarism discharged itself upon the World. The energetic inventiveness, and the restless zeal for improvements, which were the notes of the latter-day Assyrian êthos in its application to the Art of War, are attested unimpeachably by the series of bas-reliefs, found *in situ* in the royal palaces, in which the successive phases of the Assyrian military equipment and technique during the last three centuries of Assyrian history are recorded pictorially with careful precision and in minute detail.

On this evidence we can detect the following improvements between the end of the third bout, *circa* 825 B.C., and the end of the fourth bout just over two hundred years later. The mounted infantryman of Asshurnazirpal's day, who had been placed on horseback—no doubt, in imitation of the Nomads—without being relieved of the encumbrance of his infantry-man's shield, has now turned into an embryonic cataphract who has discarded the shield in exchange for a flexible cuirass. This equipment of the cavalry with body-armour has been made feasible by an improvement in the shape and material of the cuirass itself, which is now made of metal scales and is cut off at the waist, in substitution for the clumsy wadded or leathern kaftan, reaching from the neck to the knees, which had done duty for a cuirass in the earlier age. The cavalry-man's legs, which are thus left exposed, are protected in compensation by stockings reaching to the thighs and boots reaching to the calf; and the same footgear enables the infantry to operate in rough country with greater ease than in an age when sandals had been the only alternative to going barefoot. Within the same span of Time there have been a number of improvements in the war-chariots: for instance, an increase in the diameter of the wheels, in the height of the sides of the body, and in the number of the crew—the driver and the archer being now reinforced by a couple of shield-bearers. There has also been an improvement in the shape of the wicker screens from behind which the foot-archers shoot. Perhaps the greatest improvement of all, however, is one of which we are informed, not by the pictorial evidence of the bas-reliefs, but by the written word of the inscriptions; and this is the institution of a royal standing army, which was probably the work of either Tiglath-Pileser III (*regnabat* 747–727 B.C.) or Sargon (*regnabat* 722–705 B.C.). The standing army served as a nucleus, and not as a substitute, for the national militia on which the Assyrian Crown had previously depended for the recruitment of its field armies. Nevertheless the establishment of a standing army must have raised the general level of Assyrian military efficiency, and have insured that the technical improvements, mentioned above, should produce the maximum of effect.

By Asshurbanipal's time (*regnabat* 669–626 B.C.), on the eve of the great catastrophe, two centuries of steady progress in the Art of War had produced an Assyrian army which was as well prepared for every task as it was scientifically differentiated into a number of specialized arms. There were the chariotry and the demi-cataphract horse-archers; the heavy foot-archers, armoured from helmet to boots, and the light foot-archers who risked their lives in head-bands, loin-cloths, and sandals; the hoplites, armed like the heavy foot-archers, except that they carried spear and shield instead of bow and quiver; and the peltasts, likewise carrying spear and shield, but wearing, in lieu of a cuirass, a pectoral secured by crossed shoulder-straps. There was probably also a corps of engineers, for there was certainly a siege-train—not, indeed, of catapults, but of battering-rams and rolling towers—and, when these engines had done their work, and the walls of the enemy fortress had been breached, the Assyrian directors of military operations knew how to cover the storming parties with volleys of arrows from massed batteries of archers. Thus fitted out, the Assyrian army was equally ready for siege operations, for mountain warfare, or for pitched battles on the plains; and its activism in the sphere of technique was matched by an activism

in tactics and strategy. The Assyrians were firm believers in
the sovereign virtue of the offensive.

None shall be weary nor stumble among them; none shall slumber nor sleep; neither shall the girdle of their loins be loosed, nor
the latchet of their shoes be broken;

Whose arrows are sharp, and all their bows bent, their horses'
hoofs shall be counted like flint, and their wheels like a whirlwind;

Their roaring shall be like a lion, they shall roar like young
lions; yea, they shall roar and lay hold of the prey, and shall carry
it away safe, and none shall deliver it.

This was the spirit of the Assyrian army down to the last,
as was shown by the account which it gave of itself in the
Harran campaign of 610 B.C., when it was fighting for a lost
cause, with the capital city of the Empire already taken by
storm and blotted out. It will be apparent that the Assyrian
army on the eve of its annihilation was not at all in the condi-
tion of the Macedonian and Roman and Mamlūk armies in
168 B.C. and A.D. 378 and A.D. 1798. Why, then, did it suffer a
more appalling disaster than theirs? The answer is that the very
activism of the Assyrian military spirit aggravated Assyria's
doom when at last it closed in upon her.

In the first place the policy of the unremitting offensive, and
the possession of a potent instrument for putting this policy
into effect, led the Assyrian war-lords in the fourth and last
bout of their militarism to extend their enterprises and commitments far beyond the limits within which their predecessors
had kept. Assyria was subject to a perpetual prior call upon
her military resources for the fulfilment of her task as warden
of the marches of the Babylonic World against the barbarian
highlanders in the Zagros and the Taurus on the one side and
against the Aramaean pioneers of the Syriac Civilization on the
other. In her three earlier bouts of militarism she had been

content to pass from the defensive to the offensive on these
two fronts, without pressing this offensive *à outrance* and without dissipating her forces in other directions. Even so, the third
bout, which occupied the two middle quarters of the ninth
century B.C., evoked in Syria the temporary coalition of Syrian
states which checked the Assyrian advance at Qarqar in 853
B.C., and it was met in Armenia by the more formidable *riposte*
of the foundation of the Kingdom of Urartu, an ex-barbarian
military Power which now borrowed the Assyrians' culture in
order to equip itself for resisting their aggression on equal
terms. In spite of these recent warnings, Tiglath-Pileser III
(*regnabat* 746–727 B.C.), when he inaugurated the last and
greatest of the Assyrian offensives, allowed himself to harbour
political ambitions and to aim at military objectives which
brought Assyria into collision with three new adversaries—
Babylonia, Elam, and Egypt—each of whom was potentially as
great a military power as Assyria herself.

Tiglath-Pileser put a conflict with Egypt in store for his
successors when he set himself to complete the subjugation of
the petty states of Syria; for Egypt could not remain indiffer-
ent to an extension of the Assyrian Empire up to her own
Asiatic frontiers, and she was in a position to frustrate or undo
the Assyrian empire-builders' work unless and until they made
up their minds to round it off by embarking on the more formidable enterprise of subjugating Egypt herself. Tiglath-
Pileser's bold occupation of Philistia in 734 B.C. may have been
a strategic master-stroke which was rewarded by the temporary submission of Samaria in 733 and the fall of Damascus in
732. But it led to Sargon's brush with the Egyptians in 720,
and Sennacherib's in 700, on the Syro-Egyptian border; and
these inconclusive encounters led on, in their turn, to Esarhaddon's conquest and occupation of Egypt, from the Delta to the
Thebaid inclusive, in the campaigns of 675 and 674 and 671

B.C. Thereupon it became manifest that, while the Assyrians
were strong enough to rout Egyptian armies and occupy the
land of Egypt and repeat the feat, they were not strong enough
to hold Egypt down. Esarhaddon himself was once more on
the march for Egypt when death overtook him in 669; and
though the Egyptian insurrection which then broke out was
successfully suppressed by Asshurbanipal in 667, he had to reconquer Egypt once again in 663. By this time the Assyrian
Government itself seems to have realized that in Egypt it was
engaged on Psyche's Task; and when Psammetichus unobtru-
sively expelled the Assyrian garrisons in 658–651 Asshurbanipal turned a blind eye to what was happening. In thus cutting
his Egyptian losses the King of Assyria was undoubtedly wise;
yet this wisdom after the event was a confession that the energies expended on five Egyptian campaigns had been wasted;
and Asshurbanipal's withdrawal did not restore the *status quo
ante* 675 B.C.; for the loss of Egypt in the fifth decade of the
seventh century was a prelude to the loss of Syria in the next
generation.

The ultimate consequences of Tiglath-Pileser's intervention
in Babylonia were far graver than those of his forward policy
in Syria, since they led, by a direct chain of cause-and-effect,
to the catastrophe of 614–610 B.C.

This Assyrian aggression in this quarter in 745 B.C. must
have been difficult to reconcile with the treaty in which the
Assyro-Babylonian frontier had been delimited by friendly
agreement—and this along a line which was decidedly favourable to Assyria—in the opening decade of the eighth century
B.C. Probably Tiglath-Pileser justified his action on the ground
that the anarchy into which Babylonia had since fallen was
spreading to the Assyrian side of the border; and, after marching in, he appears to have received some kind of mandate from
the citizens of Babylon, who saw in this sovereign of a neigh-

bouring sedentary kingdom of kindred culture a possible pro-
tector of civic life in Babylonia against the rising tide of local
Aramaean and Chaldaean Nomadism. It may also be true that
both Tiglath-Pileser and his successors were genuinely anxious
to restrict the Assyrian commitments in Babylonia to a minimum, and to avoid annexation. Tiglath-Pileser himself in 745
left Nabopolassar, the reigning king of Babylonia, on his
throne; and it was only after Nabopolassar's death eleven years
later, and after the subsequent suppression of a consequent
Chaldaean tribal insurrection against the Assyrian protectorate,
that Tiglath-Pileser 'took the hands of Bel' in 729. This prece-
dent was followed by Shalmaneser V; but it was not followed
by Shalmaneser's successor Sargon until a second, and far more
serious, Chaldaean insurrection forced Sargon, in his turn, to
'take the hands of Bel' in 710; and, even then, the Assyrian
victor sought an understanding with the discomfited Chaldaean
arch-insurgent Merodach-Baladan. Thereafter, when Sennacherib succeeded his father Sargon in 705, he deliberately ab-
stained from assuming the Babylonian Crown; and, even when
a fresh Chaldaean insurrection necessitated his intervention in
Babylonia in 703, he conferred the Babylonian Crown first
upon an Assyrianized Babylonian prince, and then upon an
Assyrian prince who was not himself the heir to the Assyrian
Throne. It was only after the great insurrection of 694–689
that Sennacherib formally put an end to the independence of
Babylonia by installing his own son—and designated successor—
Esarhaddon as Assyrian governor-general.

These facts certainly seem to testify to an Assyrian policy
of moderation *vis-à-vis* Babylonia; but they afford still more
conclusive evidence that the policy was a failure. Again and
again the Assyrian Government's hand was forced by Chaldaean insurrections which only became more frequent and
more formidable in the face of persistent Assyrian forbearance.

And, while the Assyrian intervention did perform the miracle of conjuring order out of a Babylonian chaos, this order, so far from being achieved under an Assyrian aegis, was the by-product of an anti-Assyrian movement which steadily grew in scope and lustily throve upon defeat.

The first stage in a process which continued for a century and culminated in a Medo-Babylonian grand alliance was the political unification of all the Chaldaean tribes of Babylonia between 731 and 721 B.C. under the leadership of the Chief of Bit Yakin, Merodach-Baladan. The next stage was an alliance between the Chaldaeans and the Kingdom of Elam, whose Government had been as seriously alarmed by Tiglath-Pileser's intervention in Babylonia as the Egyptians had been alarmed by his descent upon Philistia. Thanks to this Elamite alliance, Merodach-Baladan was able to enter the City of Babylon in 721 and to reign there as king of Babylonia for some twelve years, in spite of the fact that at this stage the citizens of the capital still felt the rule of the local Nomad more irksome than that of the foreign sedentary Power. Nor was Merodach-Baladan's career at an end when he was ejected from Babylon by the armies of Sargon in 710. After his Assyrian conqueror's death in 705 we find the indefatigable Chaldaean entering into relations with the Arabs of the Shāmīyah and the Hamād, and sending an embassy across their ranges to so distant a fellow enemy of Assyria as the King of Judah, Hezekiah. Thereafter, in 703, Merodach-Baladan succeeded in re-occupying Babylon with the aid of his Elamite allies; and, although before the year was out he was ejected for the second time by force of Assyrian arms, and died a few years later as a refugee in Elam, the removal of the Chaldaean leader brought the Assyrian Government no nearer to a solution of the Chaldaean problem; for, with Elam still supporting them, the Chaldaean tribesmen successfully defied Sennacherib's efforts to put them out of action.

When the Assyrian war-lord occupied and devastated their tribal lands in Babylonia proper, they took refuge among the marshes and mud-banks at the head of the Persian Gulf; and, when in 694 he built a fleet on the Tigris, manned it with Phoenician crews, and put the Assyrian army on board in order to destroy the Chaldaeans in their aquatic fastness by amphibious operations, he merely gave the Elamites the opportunity to fall upon his line of communications, enter Babylon, and carry his puppet-king of Babylonia away captive. Nor did it profit Sennacherib when he took his revenge next year by defeating the Elamites in the field and capturing, in his turn, the puppet whom they had set upon the Babylonian Throne in his own puppet's place; for he failed to re-occupy Babylon; and the vacant throne was mounted by a man of character, Mushezib-Marduk, who succeeded in weaning the citizens of the capital from their pro-Assyrian policy.

This secession of the City of Babylon in 693 from the Assyrian to the Chaldaeo-Elamite camp was perhaps the decisive event in the long process of building up an anti-Assyrian front; for, although the Assyrians were, as usual, victorious over the combined Chaldaean and Elamite forces, and were able in the end to teach Babylon a lesson by sacking her in 689, the lesson which she learned was the opposite of that which her teachers intended. Through this impious outrage upon a city which was the cultural capital of their world, the Assyrians achieved a feat of political alchemy in Babylonia which the Babylonians could never have achieved for themselves. In the white heat of the common hatred which this Assyrian 'frightfulness' had now aroused among the ancient urban population as well as among the intrusive Nomads, citizens and tribesmen forgot the mutual antipathy which had hitherto divided them, and became fused together into a new Babylonian nation which could neither forget nor forgive what it had suffered at Assyrian

hands, and which could never rest until it had brought its oppressor to the ground.

At this penultimate stage of the long and tragic process
which Tiglath-Pileser III had unwittingly set in motion in 745
B.C., the anti-Assyrian feeling in Babylonia was so strong that
it was able to dominate, and bend to its purpose, the soul of
an Assyrian prince-of-the-blood who had been placed upon
the Babylonian Throne by *force majeure* and who was actually
the brother of the reigning king of Assyria itself. *Circa* 654
B.C. Asshurbanipal found the existence of the Assyrian Empire
threatened by a hostile coalition between the Babylonian
Crown, the Chaldaean and Aramaean tribes of the Babylonian
country-side, the Kingdom of Elam, the Northern Arabs, several South Syrian principalities, and the recently established
'successor-state' of the defunct Assyrian dominion over Egypt.
This combine of anti-Assyrian forces, which was wider than
any that had ever been brought together by Merodach-Baladan
or by Mushezib-Marduk, was headed by Asshurbanipal's own
brother, Shamash-shum-ukin; and his action will appear the
more extraordinary when we consider that by that date he had
been in peaceful occupation of the Babylonian Throne, with
Asshurbanipal's goodwill, for some fifteen years, in execution
of their father Esarhaddon's political testament. Moreover the
arch-rebel's principal ally, Elam, had just received—perhaps as
recently as the very year before Shamash-shum-ukin staked
his fortunes on her support—the heaviest defeat that had ever
yet been inflicted upon her by Assyrian arms, a defeat in which
the reigning king and his heir-apparent had been killed and
both the royal cities captured. These facts give the measure of
the strength of the Babylonian national movement that swept
Shamash-shum-ukin off his feet.

In this crisis the Assyrian army was victorious once again.
The traitor Shamash-shum-ukin escaped a worse fate by burn-

ing himself alive in his palace when Babylon was starved into surrender in 648; and *circa* 639 Elam was dealt such an annihilating blow by Assyrian arms that her derelict territory passed under the dominion of the Persian highlanders from her eastern hinterland and became the jumping-off ground from which the Achaemenidae leapt into an empty saddle when they made themselves masters of all South-Western Asia a century later. This sacrifice of the Babylonian nationalists' Assyrian and Elamite instruments in the war of 654–639 B.C. did not, however, prevent the Babylonian national movement itself from attaining its objective; for, if the Achaemenidae found the saddle empty in the sixth century, this was because the Assyrian rider had been thrown at last before the seventh century was out. Immediately after Asshurbanipal's death in 626 Babylonia revolted again under a new national leader; and this Nabopolassar completed the work which Merodach-Baladan had begun. In the new Kingdom of Media he found a more potent ally to fill the place of the defunct Kingdom of Elam; and Assyria, who had not recovered from the War of 654–639, was wiped out of existence in the War of 614–610 B.C. Even then, *in extremis*, the Assyrian army could still win victories in the field. With the help of Assyria's former vassals and present patrons the Saïtes, it drove the Babylonians back upon Harran in 610, at a stage in this war of annihilation when Harran itself as well as Nineveh and Asshur was already sacked and devastated, and when the army was fighting with its back to the Euphrates in the last unconquered corner of the Assyrian homeland; but this final victory must have been the Assyrian army's death agony, for this is the last recorded incident in the Assyrian military annals.

When we gaze back over the century and a half of ever more virulent warfare which begins with Tiglath-Pileser III's accession to the throne of Assyria in 745 B.C. and closes with a

Babylonian Nebuchadnezzar's victory over an Egyptian Necho at Carchemish in 605, the historical landmarks which stand out the most prominently at first sight are the successive 'knock-out blows' by which Assyria destroyed entire communities—razing cities to the ground and carrying whole peoples away captive. We think of the sack of Damascus in 732; the sack of Samaria in 722; the sack of Musasir in 714; the sack of Babylon in 689; the sack of Sidon in 677; the sack of Memphis in 671; the sack of Thebes in 663; the sack of Susa *circa* 639. Of all the capital cities of all the states within reach of Assyria's arm, only Tyre and Jerusalem remained inviolate on the eve of the sack of Nineveh in 612. The loss and misery which Assyria inflicted on her neighbours is beyond calculation; and yet the legendary remark of the canting schoolmaster to the boy whom he is whipping—'It hurts you less than it hurts me'—would be a more pertinent critique of Assyrian military activities than the un-ashamedly truculent and naïvely self-complacent narratives in which the Assyrian war-lords have presented their own ac-count of their performances for the instruction of Posterity.

The full and bombastic Assyrian record of victories abroad is significantly supplemented by rarer and briefer notices of troubles at home that give us some inkling of the price at which the victories were purchased; and, when we examine this domestic chronicle of Assyria at the height of her military power, we shall no longer find it strange that her victoriousness was eventually the death of her.

An increasing excess of military strain revenged itself in an increasing frequency of palace revolutions and peasant revolts. As early as the close of the second bout of aggression in the ninth century B.C. we find Shalmaneser III dying in 827 with his son on the war-path against him, and Nineveh, Asshur, and Arbela in rebellion. Asshur rebelled again in 763–762, Arrapka in 761–760, Gozan in 759; and in 746 the rebellion of Calah, the

Assyrian capital of the day, was followed by the extermination
of the ruling dynasty. Tiglath-Pileser III (*regnabat* 745–727
B.C.) was a *novus homo* who could not conceal his provenance
under the borrowed cloak of an historic name; and, if he was
also the Assyrian Marius, the Roman analogy suggests that the
establishment of a professional standing army is to be taken as
a symptom of an advanced stage of social disintegration. We
know that in the Italy of Marius' day it was the ruin of a warlike peasantry, which had been uprooted from the soil by perpetual calls to military service on ever more distant campaigns,
that made a standing army both possible and necessary—possible because there was now a reservoir of unemployed 'man-
power' to draw upon, and necessary because these men who
had lost their livelihood on the land must be provided with
alternative employment if they were to be restrained from
venting their unhappiness and resentment through the channel
of revolution. We may discern in the establishment of the Assyrian standing army a parallel attempt to find the same military solution for the same social problem. This military solution, however, was no more successful in allaying the domestic
troubles of Tiglath-Pileser's Assyria than it was in allaying
those of Marius' Italy. Tiglath-Pileser's successor Shalmaneser
V (*regnabat* 727–722 B.C.) seems to have fallen foul of the City
of Asshur, like Tiglath-Pileser's predecessors. Sennacherib in
681 was murdered by one of his own sons, who was apparently
hand in glove with the Babylonian nationalists; and we have
seen already how Asshurbanipal's throne and empire were
threatened by the action of his brother Shamash-shum-ukin,
King of Babylon, in 654, when this renegade Assyrian prince
placed himself at the head of an anti-Assyrian coalition. Therewith the two streams of domestic *stasis* and foreign warfare
merge into one; and after Asshurbanipal's death this swells into
a mighty river whose rushing waters bear Assyria away to her

now inevitable doom. During the last years of Assyrian history the domestic and the foreign aspect of Assyria's disintegration are hardly distinguishable.

The approaching doom cast its shadow over the soul of Asshurbanipal himself in his declining years.

The rules for making offerings to the dead and libations to the ghosts of the kings my ancestors, which had not been practiced, I reintroduced. I did well unto god and man, to dead and living. Why have sickness, ill-health, misery and misfortune befallen me? I cannot away with the strife in my country and the dissensions in my family. Disturbing scandals oppress me alway. Misery of mind and of flesh bow me down; with cries of woe I bring my days to an end. On the day of the City-God, the day of the festival, I am wretched; Death is seizing hold on me and bears me down. With lamentation and mourning I wail day and night; I groan: 'O God, grant even to one who is impious that he may see Thy light.' How long, O God, wilt Thou deal thus with me? Even as one who hath not feared god and goddess am I reckoned.

This confession is remarkable in its unconventionality and moving in its sincerity and even pathetic in its bewilderment, but above all it is illuminating in its blindness. When this mood overtook him, did the last of the Assyrian war-lords never find himself silently reciting that terrible catalogue of cities sacked and peoples wiped out by Assyrian arms—a list which concluded with his own sack of Susa and annihilation of Elam? Or was the burden of this memory so intolerable that the tormented militarist thrust it from him, in desperation, whenever it threatened to overwhelm him? His successor Sin-shar-ishkun, at any rate, must have lived through a moment when these haunting recollections closed in on him and would not be denied, as the Athenians were beset by the ghosts of their misdeeds when they received the news of the Battle of Aegospotami.

At Athens the disaster was announced by the arrival of the *Paralus*, and a wail spread from the Peiraeus through the Long Walls into the city as the news passed from mouth to mouth. That night no one slept. Besides mourning for the dead they mourned far more bitterly for themselves, for they expected to suffer the fate which they had inflicted upon the Melians (who were colonists of the Lacedaemonians) when they had besieged and captured their city, and upon the Histiaeans, the Scionians, the Toronians, the Aeginetans and many other Hellenic peoples. Next morning they held an assembly in which it was decided to block up all the harbours except one, to clear the fortifications for action, to dispose troops to man them, and to put the city into a thorough state of defence for the eventuality of a siege.

As the Athenian dêmos felt and acted at this dreadful moment in 405 B.C., the last king of Assyria must have felt and acted in 612 B.C., when he received the news that his Scythian allies, who had been his last hope of worldly salvation, had gone over to the enemy and that the united forces of the hostile coalition were closing in irresistibly upon Nineveh. The rest of the story is not the same in the two cases; for the Athenian dêmos capitulated and was spared by the generosity of the victors, while King Sin-shar-ishkun in Nineveh stood a siege, held out to the bitter end, and perished with his people when the city was taken by storm at the third assault. Thus the doom which Asshurbanipal had deprecated overwhelmed his successor and was not averted either by Asshurbanipal's tardy contrition or by his partial conversion from the works of War to the arts of Peace. Asshurbanipal's learned library of Babylonic literature (an Assyrian museum of a culture which an Assyrian militarism had blighted) and his exquisite bas-reliefs (designed by living Assyrian artists, and depicting the scientific slaughter of man and beast by the Assyrian military technique) had made of Nineveh by the year 612 B.C. a treasure-house which is not altogether incomparable with the Athens of 405–404. The treas-

ures of Nineveh were buried under her ruins to enrich a remote Posterity in the heyday of a civilization which does not
reckon the Babylonic Society among its forebears. But, if Nineveh perished where Athens survived, this was because Assyria
had already committed suicide before her material destruction
overtook her. The clearly attested progress of the Aramaic language at the expense of the native Akkadian in the Assyrian
homeland during the last century and a half of Assyria's existence as a state shows that the Assyrian people was being peace-
fully supplanted by the captives of the Assyrian bow and spear
in an age when the Assyrian military power stood at its zenith.
Depopulation was the price which had to be paid for militarism, and it was a price that was ultimately as ruinous for the
Assyrian army as for the rest of the Assyrian body social. The
indomitable warrior who stood at bay in the breach at Nineveh
in 612 B.C. was 'a corpse in armour,' whose frame was only held
erect by the massiveness of the military accoutrements in which
this *felo de se* had already smothered himself to death. When
the Median and Babylonian storming party reached that stiff
and menacing figure, and sent it clattering and crashing down
the moraine of ruined brickwork into the fosse below, they did
not suspect that their terrible adversary was no longer a living
man at the moment when they struck their daring, and apparently decisive, blow.

CHAPTER V

The Burden of Nineveh; Charlemagne and Timur Lenk

We have sketched our portrait of the Assyrian militarism at full length because it is the prototype of so many signal examples of the same aberration. The tableau of the 'corpse in armour' conjures up a vision of the Spartan phalanx on the battle-field at Leuctra in 371 B.C. The ironic fate of the militarist who is so intemperate in waging wars of annihilation against his neighbours that he deals unintended destruction to himself recalls the self-inflicted doom of the Carolingians or the Timurids, who built up great empires out of the agony of their Saxon or Persian victims, only to provide rich spoils for Scandinavian or Uzbeg adventurers who lived to see the empire-builders pay for their imperialism by falling from world power to impotence within the span of a single lifetime.

Another form of suicide which the Assyrian example calls to mind is the self-destruction of those militarists—be they barbarians or people of higher culture with a capacity for putting their talents to a better use—who break into, and break up, some universal state or other great empire that has been giving a spell of peace to the peoples and lands over which it has spread its aegis. The conquerors ruthlessly tear the imperial mantle into shreds in order to expose the millions of human beings whom it has sheltered to the terrors of darkness and the shadow of death, but the shadow descends inexorably upon the criminals as well as upon their victims. Demoralized on the morrow of their victory by the splendour and the vastness of their prize, these new masters of a ravished world are apt, like the Kilkenny cats, to perform 'the friendly office' for one another until not one brigand in the band is left alive to feast upon the plunder.

We may watch how the Macedonians, when they have overrun the Achaemenian Empire, and have pressed on beyond its farther frontiers into India, within the eleven years following Alexander's passage of the Hellespont, next turn their arms with equal ferocity against one another during the forty-two years intervening between Alexander's death in 323 B.C. and the overthrow of Lysimachus at Corupedium in 281 B.C. The grim performance was repeated a thousand years later in another passage of Syriac history, when the Primitive Muslim Arabs emulated—and thereby undid—the Hellenic Macedonians' work by overruning in twelve years the Roman and Sasanian dominions in South-Western Asia over almost as wide a sweep of territory as had once been conquered in eleven years by Alexander from the Achaemenidae. In this Arab case the twelve years of conquest were followed by the twenty-four years of fratricidal strife which began with the assassination of the Caliph 'Uthmān in A.D. 656 and culminated in the martyrdom of the Prophet's grandson Husayn in A.D. 680. Once again the conquerors of South-Western Asia fell on one another's swords; and the glory and profit of rebuilding a Syriac universal state which Alexander had overthrown was left to the usurping Umayyads and to the interloping 'Abbasids, instead of falling to those companions and descendants of the Prophet whose lightning conquests had prepared the way. The same spectacle is presented in the New World when the Aztecs and the Incas go down before the Spaniards. The Spanish *conquistadores* of

the Mexic and the Andean universal state overran two conti-
nents—from Florida to the Isthmus, and from the Isthmus to
Chile—only to fight over the spoils as ferociously as the companions of Muhammad or the companions of Alexander; and
the Macedonian war-lord in his grave was not so powerless to
maintain discipline among the troops that had once followed
him in the field as was a living sovereign at Madrid to impose
the king's peace upon the adventurers who paid him a nominal
allegiance on the other side of the Atlantic. The same suicidal
Assyrian vein of militarism was displayed by the barbarians
who overran the derelict provinces of a decadent Roman Empire. The Visigoths were overthrown by the Franks and the
Arabs; the smaller fry among the English 'successor-states' in
Britain were devoured by Mercia and Wessex; the Merovin-
gians were brushed aside by the Carolingians, and the Umayyads by the 'Abbasids. And this suicidal ending of our classic
example of a 'heroic age' is characteristic, in some degree, of
the latter end of all the Völkerwanderungen that have overrun
the domains of other decrepit universal states.

There is another variety of militaristic aberration of which
we shall also find the prototype in the Assyrian militarism
when we envisage Assyria, not as an artificially isolated en-
tity in herself, but in her proper setting as an integral part of
a larger body social which we have called the Babylonic Society. In this Babylonic World Assyria was invested, as we
have seen, with the special function of serving as a march
whose primary duty was to defend, not only herself, but also
the rest of the society in which she lived and had her being,
against the predatory barbarian highlanders from the east and
the north and the aggressive Aramaean pioneers of the Syriac
Civilization from the opposite quarters of the compass. In ar-
ticulating a march of this Assyrian kind out of a previously

undifferentiated social fabric, a society stands to benefit in all its members; for while the march itself is stimulated in so far as it responds successfully to the challenge—which it has now taken upon itself—of resisting external pressures, the interior—which the march now shields—is relieved of pressure in a corresponding degree, and is thereby set free to face other challenges and accomplish other tasks. This division of labour is salutary so long as the march continues to direct its specialized military prowess exclusively to its appointed task of repelling the external enemy. So long as they are used for this socially legitimate purpose, the military virtues need not be socially destructive—even though the necessity of bringing them into play at all may be a lamentable testimony to the imperfection of human nature in those generations of men who have been setting their feet upon the lower rungs of the ladder of Civilization during these last six thousand years. But these virtues, such as they are, become fatally transformed into the vice of Militarism, in the sinister sense, if ever the frontiersmen turn the arms which they have learnt to use in warfare with the outsider beyond the pale against the members of their own society whom it is their proper task to defend and not to attack.

The evil of this aberration is not so much that it exposes the society as a whole to the assaults of the external enemy whom the frontiersmen have hitherto kept at bay; for the frontiersmen seldom turn against their own kith and kin until they have established so great an ascendancy over their proper adversaries that their hands are free for other mischief and their ambitions fired for aiming at greater objectives. Indeed, when a march turns and rends the interior of its own society, it usually manages to hold the external enemy off with its left hand while it is waging a fratricidal war with its right. The deadly harm of this misdirection of military energies lies not so much in the

opening of the gates to an alien invader—though this is sometimes one of the incidental consequences in the end—as in the
betrayal of a trust and in the precipitation of an internecine
conflict between two parties whose natural relation with each
other is to dwell in unity. When a march turns against its own
interior, it is taking the offensive in what is really a civil war;
and it is notorious that civil wars are waged with greater bit-
terness and ferocity than any others. This explains the momen-
tousness of the consequences that ultimately followed from the
action of Tiglath-Pileser III in 745 B.C., when he turned his
Assyrian arms against Babylonia instead of continuing to exercise them exclusively against Nairi and Aram, which were their
legitimate field; and we shall see, from a survey of other instances which this Assyrian prototype calls to mind, that the
denouement of the ensuing Assyro-Babylonian hundred years'
war, catastrophic as it was, was not peculiar to this particular
case. The aberration of the march which turns against the interior is, in its very nature, disastrous for the society as a whole;
and it is destructive, above all, to the party which commits the
original act of outrageous behaviour. When a sheep-dog who
has been bred and trained to be the shepherd's partner lapses
into the êthos and behaviour of the wolves whom it is his duty
to chevy away, and betrays his trust by harrying the sheep on
his own account, he works far worse havoc than any genuine
wolf could work so long as a loyal sheep-dog was snapping at
his flanks; but at the same time it is not the flock that suffers
the most heavily from the catastrophe which follows the sheep-
dog's treachery. The flock is decimated but survives; the dog
is destroyed by his outraged master; and the frontiersman who
turns against his own society is dooming himself to inexorable
destruction because he is striking at the source from which his
own life springs. He is like a sword-arm that plunges the blade
which it wields into the body of which it is a member; or like

a woodman who saws off the branch on which he is sitting, and so comes crashing down with it to the ground while the mutilated tree-trunk remains still standing.

It was perhaps an intuitive sense of the perversity of this mis-direction of energies that moved the Austrasians to protest so vehemently in A.D. 754 against their war-lord Pepin's decision to respond to Pope Stephen's call to arms against their brethren the Lombards. The Papacy had turned its eyes towards this Transalpine Power, and had whetted Pepin's ambition by anointing him king in 749 and crowning him on the eve of the projected Italian expedition, because Austrasia in Pepin's gen-eration had distinguished herself by her prowess in serving as a march of Western Christendom on two fronts: against the pagan Saxon barbarians who were pushing their way towards the Rhine from the no-man's-land of Northern Europe, and against the Muslim Arab conquerors of North-West Africa and the Iberian Peninsula who were pressing on across the Pyrenees. In 754 the Austrasians were invited to divert their energies from the fields in which they had just been finding their true mission, and to inflict upon the Lombards in Italy the fate which Austrasian arms had prevented the Arabs and the Saxons from inflicting upon the Franks themselves in Gaul. The misgivings of the Austrasian rank-and-file over this Italian adventure were proved by the event to be better justified than their leader's appetite for it; for in overriding the objections of his henchmen King Pepin forged the first link in a chain of military and political commitments which bound Austrasia to Italy ever more tightly. Pepin's Italian campaigns against Ais-tulf in 755 and 756 led on to Charlemagne's Italian campaign against Desiderius in 773–4—notwithstanding the effort of Char-lemagne's mother and Pepin's widow Queen Bertrade to heal a breach between Frank and Lombard which King Pepin had opened against his people's will. When Bertrade arranged a

marriage between her own and Pepin's son, who had now succeeded his father, and the daughter of Aistulf's successor Desiderius, Charlemagne repudiated his Lombard wife Desiderata
and fulfilled his own father's ambitions by conquering his wife's
father's kingdom outright. But Charlemagne's seizure of the
Lombard Crown did not dispose of the Italian question or
relieve the Transalpine Power of its ultramontane anxieties. In
extinguishing the independence of the Lombard Kingdom
Charlemagne saddled his own house irrevocably with the burden of defending and controlling the Papacy; and his protectorate over the Ducatus Romanus involved him in more distant
complications with Lombard principalities and East Roman
outposts in the South of Italy. Even when, on the fourth of the
expeditions which he was compelled to make to Rome, he attained the apogee of his outward success in being crowned by
the Pope, and acclaimed by the Roman people, as Augustus,
the honour cost him the annoyance of a diplomatic conflict
with the Court of Constantinople which dragged on for more
than ten years.

The true verdict on Charlemagne's Italian policy is given by
the chronological table of the acts of his reign, which shows
how these ultramontane commitments repeatedly diverted him
—and this often at critical moments—from his major military
task of prosecuting the Great Saxon War. After throwing
down the gauntlet to the Saxons by marching into the heart of
their country, and hewing down the Irminsul, in 772, Charlemagne disappeared beyond the Alps during 773 and 774, and so
left the way open for the Saxons in the latter year to take reprisals on Hessen. Thereafter the would-be 'knock-out blow'
of 775–6 had to be suspended in the spring of the latter year
while the smiter of the Saxons went off on a second ultramontane expedition to put down a rebellion raised by Hrodgaud,
the Lombard Duke of Friuli. In the middle of the next and

most formidable phase of the war, in which the Saxons were
led for eight years (777–85) by Widukind—a captain whose
strategy was the offensive defensive—Charlemagne had to pay
the third visit to Italy, and second to Rome, of his reign; and
the lull in the Saxon War which followed the submission of
Widukind in 785 gave no rest to Austrasian arms, for the year
787 saw Charlemagne pay his third visit to Rome, lead an inconclusive expedition against the South Lombard Duchy of
Benevento, and impose his authority by a military demonstra-
tion upon the Lombards' old friends, and his own restive vassals, the Bavarians. The fourth and last phase of the Saxon War,
in which the conquered but uncowed barbarians made a desperate and long-drawn-out effort to throw off the Austrasian
yoke with the aid of the Frisians (*nitebantur* A.D. 792–804), was
in progress during Charlemagne's fourth visit to Rome, and
fifth to Italy, in 800–801.

This war of attrition against the Saxons grievously exhausted
the Carolingian Power. The exhaustion declared itself in the
break-up of the Carolingian Empire on the morrow of Charlemagne's death, and in the Scandinavian *revanche* for the Saxons' sufferings—a counter-attack which was opened even before
the Austrasian conqueror of the Saxons had departed this life.
It must also be remembered that the Saxon front beyond the
Rhine was not the only frontier of Western Christendom for
which Austrasia was responsible; she was likewise the warden
of the Arab frontier beyond the Pyrenees; and, when Charlemagne overthrew the Lombard Kingdom and reduced the
Bavarians to obedience, he inherited from his vanquished adversaries the wardenship of a third frontier, the Avar front beyond
the Styrian Alps. It may have been inevitable that in the second
year of his deadly duel with Widukind Charlemagne should
have been drawn away into the Transpyrenean expedition
which ended so unfortunately at Roncesvalles; but, with a

Transpyrenean as well as a Transrhenane front to hold, and with disaffection always smouldering in Aquitaine, it is evident that Charlemagne could not afford in any case to enter into new commitments on the Italian side of the Alps; and his Italian policy became suicidal when it was combined, as it was, with an ambitious forward movement on both the Transalpine fronts which the great Austrasian militarist had inherited from his forebears. It was the wantonly imposed burden of Charlemagne's five Italian expeditions that aggravated to the breaking-point the load which weighed upon Austrasia's back.

If Charlemagne broke Austrasia's back by turning her arms against the Lombard and Bavarian interior of a nascent Western Christendom when the whole of her strength was required for her terrific struggle with the Saxons beyond her Rhenish pale, Timur, in like fashion, broke the back of his own Transoxania by squandering in aimless expeditions into Iran and 'Irāq and India and Anatolia and Syria the slender reserves of Transoxanian strength which ought to have been concentrated upon Timur's proper mission of imposing his peace on the Eurasian Nomads.

In the course of nineteen years (A.D. 1362–80) of strenuous campaigning he had repulsed the attempts of the Chaghatāy Nomads to reconquer the Transoxanian oases; assumed the offensive in his turn against the foiled invaders on their native ranges in 'Mughalistan'; and rounded off his own dominions in the Eurasian march of the Iranic World by liberating the oases of Khwārizm on the Lower Oxus from the Nomads of Jūjī's appanage. Upon the completion of this great task in A.D. 1380 Timur had a greater prize within his reach—no less a prize than the succession to the Eurasian Empire of Chingis Khan—for in Timur's generation the Eurasian Nomads were in retreat on all sectors of the long frontier between the Desert and the Sown. While Timur was winning his victory over the hordes of

'Mughalistan' and Qipchāq on the sector between the Pamirs and the Caspian, the Moldavians and Lithuanians and Cossacks were cutting short the appanage of Jūjī at its opposite extremity in the great western bay of the Steppe between the Iron Gates of the Danube and the Cataracts of the Dniepr; the Muscovites were shaking off the yoke of the Qipchāq horde; and the Chinese were driving out the mongol Khāqāns—the senior branch of Chingis Khan's house, and the nominal overlords of all the Chingisid appanages—from Qubilay's capital at Peking into a no-man's-land beyond the outer face of the Great Wall from which these barbarian intruders had originally come. In every quarter the Nomads were on the run, and the next chapter in the history of Eurasia was to be a race between the resurgent sedentary peoples round about for the prize of Chingis' heritage. In this competition the Moldavians and Lithuanians were too remote to be in the running; the Muscovites were wedded to their forests and the Chinese to their fields; the Cossacks and the Transoxanians were the only competitors who had succeeded in making themselves at home on the Steppes without uprooting the sedentary foundations of their own way of life. Each in their own way, they had acquired something of the strength of Nomadism and had combined this with the strength of a sedentary civilization. To a sharp-eyed observer in A.D. 1380 it might have seemed as though the victory in the race for the dominion of Eurasia must lie between these two runners; and at that moment the Transoxanian competitor had, to all appearance, by far the better chance, for, besides being stronger in himself and nearer to the heart of the Steppe, he was also the first in the field, while, as the recognized champion of the Sunnah, he had potential partisans among the sedentary Muslim communities who were the outposts of Islam on the opposite coasts of the Steppe: in Qāzān and Krim on the one hand, and in Kansu and Shensi on the other.

For an instant Timur appeared to appreciate his opportunity and to grasp at it with determination. The civil war between rival sections of the Qipchāq horde, which had permitted Timur to conquer Khwārizm and the Muscovites to assert their independence, was duly taken advantage of by Timur for a more ambitious purpose than the mere acquisition of a single border province. He intervened in the internal affairs of Qipchāq by giving his support to one of the rival pretenders, Toqatmysh; it was thanks to Timur's aid that Toqatmysh was able in the course of the years 1378–82 to unite the whole of Jūjī's appanage under his own leadership, reduce the Muscovites to obedience again by taking and burning Moscow itself, and inflict a heavy defeat upon the Lithuanians. All this was done by Toqatmysh as Timur's vassal, and the effect was to make Timur master, directly or indirectly, of the whole western half of the Eurasian Steppe with its surrounding sedentary dependencies, from the Irtish to the Dniepr and from the Pamirs to the Urals. At this juncture, however, the Transoxanian conqueror of the Eurasian no-man's-land suddenly turned right-about, directed his arms towards the interior of the Iranic World, and devoted the remaining twenty-four years of his life to a series of barren and destructive campaigns in this quarter. Even when Toqatmysh, emboldened by seeing his suzerain fly off at a tangent, unintentionally drew him back into his proper field through an act of audacious aggression, Timur obstinately resumed his new course as soon as he had disposed of the nuisance in Qipchāq in a winter campaign across the Steppes which was the most brilliant and characteristic *tour de force* in the Transoxanian captain's whole history.

A brief exposition of the annals of the last twenty-four years of Timur's life will show how persistently, throughout that span of nearly a quarter of a century, he rejected an opportunity which he had held in the hollow of his hand at the mo-

ment of transition from the first to the second phase of his
career.

Timur spent the seven years 1381–7 in conquering Iran and
Transcaucasia, save for a single punitive expedition in 1383–4
against a still recalcitrant Chaghatāy Khan in 'Mughalistan.' He
did not even take warning from a brush between his own
troops and Toqatmysh's which occurred in 1385 in Azerbaijan;
and at the beginning of 1388 he was in Fars, on the point of
rounding off his conquest of the Iranian Plateau, when he was
urgently recalled to Samarqand by Toqatmysh's invasion of
Khwārizm and Transoxania. His crushing victory over Toqatmysh at Urtapa, on the opposite coast of the Qipchāq Steppe,
in 1391 replaced in Timur's hands the opportunity which he
had held in 1380 and had neglected since 1381. This time it was
in his power to make himself the direct master of Qipchāq and
all its dependencies. Moreover, after his triumphal return to
Samarqand from Qipchāq at the beginning of 1392, he was able
to stamp out the last embers of revolt in 'Mughalistan' and to
establish his suzerainty definitively over the Chaghatāy horde.
Eurasia now lay at his feet; but instead of stooping to pick up
the prize he rode off again, that summer, in the opposite direction, made straight for Fars—that is to say, for the point on his
course at which he had been compelled to desist from the conquest of South-Western Asia in 1388—and proceeded systemati-
cally with the subjugation of 'Irāq and Armenia and Georgia.
In the course of this famous 'Five Years' Campaign' (July
1392–July 1396) Timur once again was drawn, in spite of himself, out of his intended course by a fresh incursion of Toqatmysh into Transcaucasia in the spring of 1395. Timur's counter-
stroke carried him across the Caucasus and the Terek and the
Steppes into Muscovy; but in 1396 he retraced his steps from
Qipchāq to South-Western Asia, and returned to Samarqand
across Iran.

From the summer of 1396 to the spring of 1398 Timur rested at Samarqand from his devastating labours; but this pause was not followed by a consolidation or extension of his hold upon Eurasia. Having now completed the pulverization of the heart of the Iranic World (of which he was himself a child), he set himself next to harry, in turn, its south-eastern and north-western extremities, where the Taghlāqī princes of Hindustan and the 'Osmanlī princes of Rūm were at that time extending the Iranic domain at the expense of the Hindu World and Orthodox Christendom respectively. Timur's amīrs objected to crossing the Hindu Kush and attacking their own Turkish kinsmen and co-religionists in India as strongly as the henchmen of Pepin had once objected, in similar circumstances, to crossing the Alps and attacking their Lombard kinsmen in Italy; but Timur, like Pepin, made his own will prevail. The Indian campaign kept him occupied from the spring of 1398 to the spring of 1399; and by the autumn of the latter year he was off again on what was destined to be the most famous, though it was not really the most brilliant, chapter of his military career: a second five years' campaign which included his encounter with the Maghribī philosopher Ibn Khaldūn at Damascus in 1401 and his defeat and capture of the Ottoman Sultan Bāyezīd Yilderim in 1402.

Returning to Samarqand in the July of 1404, Timur was on the war-path again by November; and now at last, for the first time in twenty-three years, his face was deliberately set in an auspicious direction; for his objective, this time, was China; and although it may be doubted, in the light of his record in South-Western Asia, whether he would have repeated the Mongols' feat of conquering China outright—a task which it had taken even the Mongols seventy years (A.D. 1207–77) to complete—nevertheless this latest enterprise of Timur's, had he lived to carry it out, might have had enduring consequences of historical importance; for even a passing raid on China might have left Timur in permanent possession of the eastern sectors of the southern border of the Eurasian Steppe from the Tarim Basin to Manchuria; and that would have placed the whole of the Steppe in his power. At this point, however, we pass into the realm of conjecture; for even a militarist who was favoured with Timur's lucky star could not throw away twenty-three years with impunity. On his China campaign he had marched no farther eastward than Utrār before Death overtook him.

Timur's self-stultification is a supreme example of the suicidalness of Militarism, as will appear from a comparison between his fiasco and Charlemagne's.

In both cases the attempt of the march to conquer the interior was ephemeral—and indeed it is seldom that a relatively backward community does succeed in assimilating to itself by the crude expedient of military conquest another community which is in advance of it on the same path of civilization. Like the Transoxanian domination which Timur imposed by force of arms upon Iran and 'Irāq, the Austrasian domination which Charlemagne imposed upon Lombardy and Bavaria faded away after the conqueror's death. Yet the effects of Charlemagne's militarism were not altogether transient; for his empire held together in some fashion for three-quarters of a century after his own hand was removed; and the destinies of its several parts were permanently modified through their union into a single body social which lived on, in the shape of a *Respublica Christiana*, long after the evaporation of the military force by which the union had originally been brought about. By contrast, Timur's empire was not only shorter-lived than Charlemagne's but was also without any social after-effects of a positive kind. West of the Caspian Gates it dissolved in A.D. 1405 upon the news of Timur's death; in Khurāsān and Transoxania it broke up into weak and warring fragments after Shah Rukh's death

in A.D. 1446; and the only traceable after-effect is wholly negative. In sweeping away everything that it found in its path, in
order to rush headlong to its own destruction, Timur's imperialism simply created a political and social vacuum in South-
Western Asia; and this vacuum eventually drew the 'Osmanlis
and the Safawis into a collision which dealt the stricken Iranic
Society its death-blow.

Again, Charlemagne's diversion of Austrasian military energies from the frontiers of Western Christendom to the interior
was fatal to Austrasia herself without proving equally fatal to
the society of which Austrasia was a part. The expansion of the
Western Christendom at the expense of the continental European barbarians was eventually taken up and carried on, from
the line at which Charlemagne had come to a halt, by the descendants of Charlemagne's Saxon victims, and her expansion
at the expense of the Syriac World in the Iberian Peninsula by
a number of local Western Christian principalities, several of
which were direct 'successor-states' of the Carolingian Empire.
On both these fronts the price that the Western Christendom
had to pay for Charlemagne's militarism was a pause which
lasted for rather less than two centuries, and which was then
followed by three centuries (*circa* A.D. 975–1275) of further
advance. On the other hand Timur's militarism deprived the
Iranic Society for ever of its Promised Land in Eurasia.

The Iranic Society's forfeiture of the heritage of the Nomad
World declared itself first on the plane of religion. Throughout
the four centuries ending in Timur's generation Islam had been
progressively establishing its hold over the sedentary peoples
round the coasts of the Eurasian Steppe and had been captivat-
ing the Nomads themselves whenever they trespassed out of
the Desert on to the Sown. In the tenth century of the Christian Era, when the military and political power of the Muslim
sovereigns of the 'Abbasid Caliphate was in dissolution, their

religion was conquering the sedentary Turkish peoples on the Middle Volga and in the oases of the Tarim Basin and the Nomad Turkish followers of the Saljūq and the Ilek Khans on the Transoxanian fringe of the Steppe between the Sea of Aral and Lake Balkash. Even in the last and greatest eruption of the post-'Abbasid Völkerwanderung, when the Steppe was convulsed to its depths and discharged upon Dār-al-Islām a horde of Nomads who had never been touched by the radiation of the Islamic culture and who were prejudiced against Islam, when they encountered it, by their tincture of Nestorian Christianity, the injury which Islam sustained from the spasmodic persecution to which it was subjected by the early Mongol Khāqāns was more than counterbalanced by the unintentional service which it received from the Mongols' policy of deliberately intermixing the peoples and cultures of their vast and heterogeneous empire. It was thanks to these pagan Nomad war-lords that Islam was propagated into China—and this not only into the north-western provinces adjoining the older Islamic domain in the Tarim Basin, but also into the new province of Yunnan in the far south-west, which was carved out of a barbarian no-man's-land and added to China by Mongol arms. Thereafter, when at the turn of the thirteenth and fourteenth centuries of the Christian Era the three western appanages of the Mongol Empire—the house of Hulāgū in Iran and the house of Jūjī on the Qipchāq Steppe and the house of Chaghatāy in Transoxania and Zungaria—were converted to Islam one after another, it looked as though nothing could now prevent Islam from becoming the religion of all Eurasia; and, by the time when Timur arose as the champion of the Sunnah in Transoxania, a Muslim 'Diasporà' which had seeded itself round the western and southern coasts of the Steppe had prepared the ground—as we have noticed already—for him to reap the harvest of a Pan-Eurasian Islamic empire. It is the more significant

that the propagation of Islam in Eurasia, which had made such
headway down to Timur's time, came to a dead halt thereafter.
The only subsequent gain that Islam made in this quarter was
the conversion of the Turkish Khanate of Western Siberia at
some date shortly before the Cossack conquest in A.D. 1582; and
this success in one remote and backward corner was little for
Islam to boast of in a generation which saw another of the
'higher religions' captivate all the rest of the Eurasian Nomads
who had hitherto remained in their primitive paganism.

The outstanding religious event in Eurasia at the turn of the
sixteenth and seventeenth centuries of the Christian Era was
the conversion of the Mongols (in A.D. 1576–7) and their west-
erly kinsmen the Calmucks (*circa* A.D. 1620) to the Lamaistic
form of Mahayanian Buddhism; and this astonishing triumph
of a fossilized relic of the religious life of the long extinct In-
dic culture gives some measure of the extent to which the pres-
tige of Islam had fallen in the estimation of the Eurasian Nomads during the two centuries that had elapsed since Timur's
day.

On the political plane the Iranic culture which Timur had
first championed and then betrayed proved equally bankrupt.
The sedentary societies which did, in the end, perform the feat
of taming the Eurasian Nomadism politically were the Russian
branch of the Orthodox Christian Society and the Chinese
branch of the Far Eastern; and the sentence of servitude which
Fate had pronounced upon the Nomads when Timur made his
winter-passage across the Steppe and overthrew Toqatmysh at
Urtapa in A.D. 1391 was never executed by Transoxanian hands.
It was confirmed when, in the middle of the seventeenth century, the Cossack servants of Muscovy and the Manchu masters of China ran into each other as they were feeling their way
in opposite directions round the northern edge of the Steppe,
and fought their first battle for dominion over Eurasia in the

neighbourhood of Chingis Khan's ancestral pastures in the upper basin of the Amur. The partition of Eurasia and the subjugation of its ancient Nomad occupants by the same pair of competitors was completed a century later when the Emperor Ch'ien Lung (*imperabat* A.D. 1735–96) broke the power of the Zungar Calmucks in A.D. 1755 and gave asylum to the already broken Torgut Calmuck refugees from the dominions of the Tsar in A.D. 1771. Therewith the latest tidal wave of the Eurasian Nomadism was spent; and when the Muscovite and the Manchu Power had divided the allegiance of the Qāzāqs—the flotsam and jetsam of the latest wave but one, who were now drifting sluggishly over the eastern portion of the Qipchāq Steppe, between the Irtish and the Yaik—the whole of Eurasia, up to the northern outskirts of the Transoxanian oases, found itself under either Russian or Chinese control.

Nor did the injury inflicted by Timur's militarism upon the Iranic World, including the conqueror's own Transoxanian homeland, stop short at the loss of a potential field for expansion across and around the Eurasian Steppe. The conclusive condemnation of the destructive militarism which possessed Timur during the last twenty-four years of his career is to be found in the fact that, besides being barren in itself, it actually led in the fulness of Time—as its consequences worked themselves out in the third and fourth generation—to the undoing of the constructive work to which Timur had devoted himself for nineteen years before he ran amok in A.D. 1381. The liberator of the nascent Iranic Society in Transoxania spent the rest of his life in so recklessly wearing out the energies which he had first mobilized against a Nomad intruder that the world which he had made safe against the hordes of Chaghatāy and Jūjī found itself exposed, within little more than a hundred years after the death of the liberator-turned-militarist, to a recurrence of the Nomad peril in the shape of the Uzbegs; and

in this emergency the epigoni of Timur's house were impotent
—heirs, as they were, to the debilitating social legacy of Timur's military excesses—to repeat their ancestor's original feat.
The Uzbeg 'drive' at the heart of the Iranic World was eventually arrested, not by any Timurid prince of Farghānā or
Khurāsān, but by the new Safawī Power of Shah Ismā'īl; and
even Shah Ismā'īl's arms, which did effectively bar the Uzbegs'
farther progress, were unable to drive the intruders right back
into the Eurasian no-man's-land out of which they had issued.
With his relatively distant base of operations in Azerbaijan and
with his grandiose ambitions on the west—ambitions which involved him in an unequal contest with the 'Osmanlis—his power
to play the liberator on the eastern front was limited; and after
expelling the Uzbegs once for all from Khurāsān he was compelled in the end to leave them in permanent possession of
Transoxania.

Thus, a century and a half after the year in which Timur
had girded himself to liberate his country from the dominion
of the Chaghatāy horde, Transoxania fell under the yoke of another swarm of Nomads, from the back-of-beyond, who were
even more barbarous than the hateful and contemptible 'Jātah';
and under this yoke the former Eurasian march of the Iranic
World, which had once spread her terror as puissantly as Assyria, was destined to lie prostrate and passive for the next
three hundred and fifty years, until, in the third quarter of the
nineteenth century of the Christian Era, the long-ground-down
peasantry of the Transoxanian oases obtained at last the allevi-
ation of exchanging an Uzbeg for a Russian master.

It is a curious reflection that, if Timur had not turned his
back on Eurasia and his arms against Iran in A.D. 1381, the present relations between Transoxania and Russia might have been
the inverse of what they actually are. In those hypothetical circumstances Russia to-day might have found herself included in

an empire of much the same extent as the area of the Soviet Union but with quite a different centre of gravity—an Iranic Empire in which Samarqand would be ruling Moscow instead of Moscow ruling Samarqand. This imaginary picture of an alternative course of Iranic history may appear outlandish because the actual course has been taking an altogether different direction for the last four hundred years and more. At least as strange a picture will unfold itself before our mind's eye if we plot out an alternative course of Western history in which the consequences of Charlemagne's militarism for our world are imagined to have been as utterly disastrous as those of Timur's militarism actually were for his. On this analogy we shall have to picture Austrasia being submerged by the Magyars and Neustria by the Vikings in the tenth century, and the heart of the Carolingian Empire remaining thereafter under this barbarian domination until in the fourteenth century the 'Osmanlis step in to impose the lesser evil of an alien civilization upon these derelict marches of Western Christendom.

Thus, besides forfeiting a Promised Land, Timur undid his own work of liberating his native country; but the greatest of all his acts of destruction was committed against himself. He has succeeded in making his name immortal at the price of erasing from the minds of Posterity all memory of the deeds for which he might have been remembered for good. To how many people in either Christendom or Dār-al-Islām to-day does Timur's name call up the image of a champion of Civilization against Barbarism, who led the clergy and people of his country to a hard-won victory at the end of a nineteen-years-long struggle for independence? To the vast majority of those to whom the name of Timur Lenk or Tamerlane means anything at all, it commemorates a militarist who perpetrated as many horrors in the span of twenty-four years as had been perpetrated in a century by a succession of Assyrian kings from

Tiglath-Pileser III to Asshurbanipal inclusive. We think of the monster who razed Isfarā'in to the ground in 1381; built two thousand prisoners into a living mound, and then bricked them over, at Sabzawār in 1383; piled 5,000 human heads into minarets at Zirih in the same year; cast his Lūrī prisoners alive over precipices in 1386; massacred 70,000 people, and piled the heads of the slain into minarets, at Isfahān in 1387; massacred the garrison of Takrit, and piled their heads into minarets, in 1393; massacred 100,000 prisoners at Delhi in 1398; buried alive the 4,000 Christian soldiers of the garrison of Sivas after their capitulation in 1400; built twenty towers of skulls in Syria in 1400 and 1401; and dealt with Baghdad in 1401 as he had dealt fourteen years earlier with Isfahān. In minds which know him only through such deeds, Timur has caused himself to be confounded with the ogres of the Steppe—a Chingis and an Attila and the like—against whom he had spent the better half of his life in waging a Holy War. The crack-brained megalomania of the homicidal madman whose one idea is to impress the imagination of Mankind with a sense of his military power by a hideous abuse of it is brilliantly conveyed in the hyperboles which the English poet Marlowe has placed in the mouth of his Tamburlaine:

> I hold the Fates bound fast in yron chaines,
> And with my hand turne Fortune's wheel about,
> And sooner shall the Sun fall from his Spheare,
> Than Tamburlaine be slaine or overcome . . .
> The God of war resignes his roume to me,
> Meaning to make me Generall of the world;
> Jove, viewing me in armes, lookes pale and wan,
> Fearing my power should pull him from his throne.
> Where ere I come the fatall sisters sweat,
> And griesly death by running to and fro,
> To doo their ceassles homag to my sword . . .
> Millions of soules sit on the bankes of Styx,

Waiting the back returne of Charon's boat,
Hell and Elysian swarme with ghosts of men,
That I have sent from sundry foughten fields,
To spread my fame through hell and up to heaven . . .
Nor am I made Arch-monark of the world,
Crown'd and invested by the hand of Jove,
For deeds of bounty or nobility;
But since I exercise a greater name,
The Scourge of God and terrour of the world,
I must apply my selfe to fit those tearmes,
In war, in blood, in death, in crueltie . . .
I will persist a terrour to the world,
Making the Meteors, that like armèd men
Are seene to march upon the towers of heaven,
Run tilting round about the firmament,
And breake their burning Lances in the aire,
For honor of my woondrous victories.

In analyzing the careers of Timur and Charlemagne and the
kings of Assyria from Tiglath-Pileser III to Asshurbanipal, we
have observed the same phenomenon in all three cases. The
military prowess which a society develops among its frontiersmen for its defence against external enemies undergoes a sinister transformation into the moral malady of Militarism when
it is diverted from its proper field in the no-man's-land beyond
the pale and is turned against the frontiersmen's own brethren
in the interior of a world which it is their mission to protect
and not to devastate. A number of other examples of this destructive social evil will readily occur to our minds.

We shall think of Mercia turning against the other English
'successor-states' of the Roman Empire in Britain the arms
which she had sharpened in the performance of her original
function as the English march against Wales; of the Plantag-
enet Kingdom of England attempting in the Hundred Years'
War to conquer the sister Kingdom of France instead of at-
tending to her proper business of enlarging the bounds of their

common mother, Latin Christendom, at the expense of 'the Celtic Fringe'; and of the Norman King Roger of Sicily turning his military energies to the extension of his dominions in Central Italy—at the expense of the South Lombard duchies and the Holy Roman Empire and the States of the Church—instead of devoting himself to carrying on his forebears' work of enlarging the bounds of Western Christendom in the Mediterranean at the expense of Orthodox Christendom and Dār-al-Islām. In the Mexic World we see the Aztecs warring down the Toltecs, to whom they owed their own initiation into the Mexic culture, instead of confining themselves to their proper task of guarding the northern march against the unconverted Chichimecs of the wilderness; in the Andean World we see the Incas bending their energies to the subjugation of their lowland neighbours in the coast-lands and their highland neighbours in Ecuador, who were co-heirs with them in the heritage of the Andean Civilization, while they made little headway against the dangerous savages of Amazonia or the valiant barbarians of Southern Chile and the Pampas, whom it was their mission to keep at bay. In like fashion the Mycenaean outposts of the Minoan Civilization on the European mainland misused the prowess which they had acquired in holding their own against the continental barbarians, in order to turn and rend their mother Crete; and the Macedonians and the Romans, whose function in the Hellenic World was to serve as wardens of the marches against the same barbarians, committed in their turn the same crime as the Mycenaeans when they contended with their neighbours, and finally with each other, for the illegitimate prize of a Pan-Hellenic hegemony. In the Sinic World the part of Rome was played by Ts'in, the western march against the barbarian highlanders of Shensi and Shansi and against the Nomads of the Eurasian Steppe, when her princes stepped into an arena which had formed itself in the interior and there eventually delivered the 'knock-out blow' in the struggle between the contending states.

In the Egyptiac World the classic Southern March in the section of the Nile Valley immediately below the First Cataract trained itself in arms, in the execution of its duty of damming back the Nubian barbarians up-river, only to turn right-about, direct its arms down-river against the Egyptiac communities in the interior, and take advantage of its military superiority in order to establish by brute force the United Kingdom of the Two Crowns. This act of Militarism, which was at once the making and the marring of the Egyptiac Civilization, has been depicted by its perpetrator, with all the frankness of self-complacency, in one of the earliest of the Egyptiac records that have come into the hands of our modern Western archaeologists. The palette of Narmer portrays the triumphant return of the Upper Egyptian war-lord from the conquest of Lower Egypt. Swollen to a superhuman stature, the royal conqueror marches behind a strutting file of standard-bearers towards a double row of decapitated enemy corpses, while below, in the image of a bull, he tramples upon a fallen adversary and batters down the walls of a fortified town. The accompanying script is believed to enumerate a booty of 120,000 human captives, 400,000 oxen, and 1,422,000 sheep and goats.

In this gruesome work of an archaic Egyptiac art we have the whole tragedy of Militarism as it has been acted over and over again since Narmer's time by the Sennacheribs and Tamerlanes and Charlemagnes of twenty different civilizations down to our own militarists in the Western World of to-day. Perhaps the most poignant of all the performances of this tragedy during its run of some six thousand years up to date is that of which Athens was guilty when she transformed herself from a 'liberator of Hellas' into a 'tyrant city' by misusing for the oppression of her Hellenic allies and protégées the naval power with which she had armed herself so short a time before in order to save herself—and rescue all Hellas in the act—from the aggression of the Achaemenidae. This Athenian aberration brought upon the whole of Hellas, as well as upon Athens herself, the never-retrieved disaster of 431–404 B.C. And, if an Athens under arms succumbed to so gross a sin, with such fatal consequences, can any of those military and naval Powers of our modern Western World who surpass Athens in arms as signally as they fall short of her in the arts, feel sure of preserving their own moral integrity?

In all the examples of which we have just been reminding ourselves in a cursory review, the suicidalness of Militarism is as evident as it is in the three classic cases with which we have dealt at greater length; and it comes out most strikingly of all where the fatal change of front has not been exclusively devastating in its effects, but has also been incidentally constructive. The diversion of Athenian and Macedonian arms from the external frontier towards the interior of the Hellenic World was disastrous for Hellas even though the Athenian and Macedonian militarists were doing something to provide the Hellenic Society with the political world order of which it then stood in need. The corresponding changes of front which were made by Rome and Ts'in and the Incas were likewise disastrous to their respective societies in spite of the fact that in each of these cases the militarist community did succeed, through the triumph of its militarism, in providing its society with a universal state. And Narmer's change of front from up-stream to down-stream in the Nile Valley had a sinister effect upon the subsequent course of Egyptiac history even though it resulted in the establishment of the United Kingdom. In the palette of Narmer we have the first evidence of that brutal vein in the Egyptiac êthos which so soon arrested the growth of the Egyptiac Civilization. The descendants of the Lower Egyptian peasants whom Narmer had slaughtered or enslaved were those unfortunate human beings who were converted into 'man-power' by the Pyramid-Builders.

The military field which we have been surveying in this chapter is illuminating for the study of the fatal chain of 'sur-feit,' 'outrage,' and 'disaster,' because military skill and prowess are edged tools which are apt to inflict fatal injuries upon those who venture to wield them if there is even the slightest clumsi-ness or misjudgement in their use. When an individual or a government or a community that has command of military power mistakes the limits of the field within which this power can be used with effect, or misconceives the nature of the ob-jectives which it is possible to attain by means of it, the disas-trousness of this aberration can hardly fail to make itself con-spicuous through the seriousness of the practical consequences. But what is palpably true of military action is also true of other human activities in less hazardous fields where the train of gunpowder that leads from 'surfeit' through 'outrage' to 'disas-ter' is not so explosive. Whatever the human faculty, or the sphere of its exercise, may be, the presumption that because a faculty has proved equal to the accomplishment of a limited task within its proper field it may therefore be counted upon to produce some inordinate effect in a different set of circum-stances is never anything but an intellectual and a moral aber-ration and never leads to anything but certain disaster.

CHAPTER VI

The Intoxication of Victory

One of the more general forms in which the tragedy of 'surfeit,' 'outrage,' and 'disaster' presents itself is in the intoxication of victory—whether the struggle in which the fatal prize is won be a war of arms or a conflict of spiritual forces. Both variants of this drama may be illustrated from the history of Rome: the intoxication of a military victory from the breakdown of the Republic in the second century B.C., the intoxication of a spiritual victory from the breakdown of the Papacy in the thirteenth century of the Christian Era.

The demoralization to which the governing class in the Roman Republic succumbed at the close of half a century of titanic warfare (220–168 B.C.), which had begun with the terrible ordeal of the Hannibalic War and had ended in the conquest of the World, is caustically described by a contemporary Greek observer who happened to be one of the victims.

The first result of the friendship between Polybius and Scipio Aemilianus was a dynamic enthusiasm for higher things which took possession of them both and which inspired them with the ambition to win moral distinction and to compete victoriously in this field with their contemporaries. The great prize on which they had thus set their hearts would have been difficult to attain in ordinary circumstances; but unhappily in the Rome of that generation the standard of the competition was lowered by the general demoralization of Society. Some were 'all out' for women,

others for unnatural vice, and many for 'shows' and drink and all
the extravagance for which 'shows' and drink gave occasion. These
were all vices for which the Greeks had a weakness, and the
Romans had caught this infirmity from them instantaneously during the Third Romano-Macedonian War. So violent and so uncon-
trolled was the passion for these vices that had overcome the
younger generation of Romans that it was quite a common thing
to buy a boy-favourite for a talent and a jar of caviare for three
hundred drachmae—behaviour which drew from Marcus Cato in
a public speech the indignant exclamation that the demoralization
of Roman Society was glaringly exposed in the mere fact of hand-
some boys fetching a higher price than land, and jars of caviare
than live-stock. If it is asked why this social malady 'lighted up'
at this particular time, two reasons can be given in answer. The
first reason was that, with the overthrow of the Kingdom of
Macedon, the Romans felt that there was no Power now left in
the World that could challenge their own supremacy. The second reason was that the material display, both private and public,
of life in Rome had been enormously enhanced by the removal to
Rome of properties from Macedonia.[1]

This was the moral pass to which the Roman governing class
had been brought by the overwhelming victory which had descended upon the Republic after years of agony in which she
had been tottering on the verge of an abyss. The first reaction
of a generation which had lived through this bewildering experience was a blind presumption that a victor's irresistible
material power was the key to a solution of all human problems, and that the only conceivable end of Man was an un-
bridled enjoyment of the grossest pleasures which this power
could place within his grasp. The victors did not realize that
this very state of mind bore witness to the moral defeat which
a militarily vanquished Hannibal had succeeded in inflicting
upon them. They did not perceive that the world in which
they passed for victors was a world in ruins, and that their own

[1] Polybius: *An Oecumenical History*, Book XXXI, ch. 25.

ostensibly victorious Roman Republic was the most sorely stricken of all the prostrate states of which this ruined world was made up. In this moral aberration they wandered in the wilderness for more than a hundred years; and in this awful century they inflicted one calamity after another upon a world which their victory had placed at their mercy, and the greatest calamities of all upon themselves.

Even in the military coin which was their own chosen currency their bankruptcy soon became manifest. The hard-won Roman triumphs over a Hannibal and a Perseus were followed by a series of humiliating Roman reverses at the hands of antagonists who were utterly outmatched by Rome in military strength: the broken, disarmed, and almost defenceless Carthage upon whom the Roman Government passed a cold-blooded sentence of annihilation in 149 B.C.; the barbarian Numantines who defied all Roman efforts to subjugate them from 153 to 133; the enslaved and expatriated Orientals who broke out of their ergastula on the Sicilian plantations in 135 and 104; the mutinous gladiators at whose head Spartacus ranged as freely over Italy from 73 to 71 as Hannibal himself had ranged from 218 to 211; the 'Citizens of the Sun' who put their faith in Aristonicus of Pergamum and held out against the power of Rome for three years (132–130) in the strength of their belief in the coming of a new dispensation; and the rebellious native princes—a Jugurtha and a Mithradates—who repudiated their allegiance and taxed their outraged suzerain's strength to the uttermost before she succeeded in bringing them to book.

The reason why Rome thus covered herself with military dishonour on the morrow of a military triumph was because during this century her officers were leading soldiers who had no longer anything to gain by victory against an enemy who, on his side, had no longer anything to hope for from laying down his arms. Both the mobilization of the Italian peasantry and the subjugation of the barbarians and the Orientals were now being exploited heartlessly for the pecuniary profit of the Roman governing class. The provinces were being drained of their inanimate wealth and their human inhabitants in order to provide lucrative contracts for Roman business men and cheap man-power for Roman senators' cattle-ranches and plantations; and the land which was being stocked with this alien slave-labour in order to multiply the fortunes of a small class of already rich men was Italian land which was being placed at the disposition of these capitalists by the impoverishment and eviction of the former peasant proprietors. The nucleus of the latifundia which 'ruined Italy' was the devastated area in the South which became public property as a result of the Hannibalic War, partly in punishment for the defection of the original owners to the invader's camp, and partly because the original owners had simply disappeared. Thereafter the new class of post-war 'planters' and 'ranchers' was able to add field to field by buying up the freeholds which were thrown upon the market when their owners were mobilized and kept under arms for years on end in some distant theatre of chronic frontier-warfare—on the western borders of the two provinces in Spain, or on the northern borders of the province of Macedonia.

In this age the subjects and the citizens of the Roman Republic were fellow victims of a *ci-devant* Roman governing class which had been transmuted by the intoxication of victory into a band of robbers. In 104 B.C., when the whole Hellenic World was overshadowed by the common menace of a barbarian avalanche from Northern Europe, the King of Bithynia, which was officially a friendly state under Rome's protectorate, could reply with biting irony, when the highest representative of the Roman Government served him with a requisition for a contingent of troops, 'that most of his subjects had been kidnapped by the [Roman] tax-farmers and were now living in

slavery in territories under Roman administration.' And in 133
B.C. a high-minded young Roman aristocrat who attempted to
carry out a social reform, and thereby precipitated a revolution, could declare without contradiction:

The wild animals that range over Italy have a hole, and each of
them has its lair and nest, but the men who fight and die for Italy
have no part or lot in anything but the air and the sunlight . . .
It is for the sake of other men's wealth and luxury that these go
to the wars and give their lives. They are called the lords of the
World, and they have not a single clod of earth to call their own.

The militant refusal of Tiberius Gracchus' peers to support
him in seeking a remedy for the Roman peasantry's wrongs
evoked a revolution which festered into a civil war; and the
self-destructive violence which was let loose within the bosom
of the Roman Commonwealth by the murder of the would-be
reformer in 133 B.C. was brought under control again only by
the establishment of the *Pax Augusta* in 31 B.C. after the Battle
of Actium.

The *Pax Augusta* inaugurated no 'Golden Age,' but only an
'Indian Summer.' The injury which Roman outrages had already inflicted upon Rome herself, and upon the whole of the
Hellenic Society, was quite past repair. The most that the gods
of the dominant minority were able to grant to the last of their
favourites was a respite which was not a reprieve; and even this
respite was to redound to the benefit, not of the bankrupt gods'
own people, but of a *nova progenies:* a 'coming race' whose eyes
were set upon a distant horizon and whose faith was founded
on the power of a different saviour. The irreparable event
which had occurred in the Hellenic World between the generation of Polybius and the generation of Virgil was the Secession of the Proletariat; and the inexorable event which was to

follow between the generation of Virgil and that of Marcus Aurelius was the budding, within the bosom of this Proletariat, of the germ of a new social order.

The material grievance which Gracchus had sought to remedy by political action was eventually redressed in a perversely anti-social way when the descendants of such Italian peasants as had succeeded in still clinging to the land were ruthlessly evicted by a succession of revolutionary war-lords, from Sulla to Augustus himself, in order to provide allotments for the descendants of their uprooted brothers who had long since become incapable of effectively 'going back to the land' after having been forced for years on end to make the camp their home and the sword their means of livelihood. This travesty of the Gracchan remedy was even worse than the disease of an uprooted and militarized citizen-proletariat. It dealt the final blow to Italian agriculture. But, at a moment when the social problems of Italy were utterly defeating all the manœuvres of Roman statesmanship, the parable of the wild things' 'holes' and 'nests,' which Tiberius Gracchus had once employed in a political speech as a figurative search-light to show up a social wrong, was being applied to illustrate a different and a deeper truth by a prophet in Syria who made no impression on the minds of the Roman authorities of the day (not even when, in the course of their administrative routine, they had occasion to put him to death). When Jesus took upon himself the sufferings of a Galilaean peasantry who had been despoiled by the same predatory hand as the peasants of the Ager Mantuanus, and when he said to the scribe 'the foxes have holes and the birds of the air have nests but the Son of Man hath not where to lay his head,' he was using the Gracchan image in order to make the Proletariat understand that the wrongful and violent spoliation of their material goods was not a ground for revolutionary reprisals, or even perhaps for political reforms, but was actually a blessing in disguise because it was an unsuspected source of spiritual wealth.

Blessed are the meek, for they shall inherit the Earth . . .
Blessed are they which are persecuted for righteousness' sake, for theirs is the Kingdom of Heaven.

In a lesser degree this intoxication of victory, which carried the Roman governing class to perdition after their conquest of the Hellenic World in the half-century ending in the Battle of Pydna, was likewise the ruin of the Spaniards and the Portuguese after their conquest of the New World at the beginning of the Modern Age of our Western history, and again the ruin of the British after their conquest of Bengal and Canada in the Seven Years' War.

The Spaniards and Portuguese, who in A.D. 1493 had obtained from the Pope an arbitral award, partitioning between them the whole of the Overseas World as though no other claimants were in the field, saw their monopoly broken within less than a century when the Dutch and the English and the French made free with the Spanish preserves in America and the Portuguese preserves in Africa and India, and both the Iberian Powers' preserves in the Far East, after the defeat of the Spanish Armada. And the intoxication of the Iberian pioneers with their original achievement—their overweening pride in the knowledge that

> We were the first that ever burst
> Into that silent sea—

was the gaping joint in their armour through which their lynx-eyed and nimble-handed European competitors directed their disabling thrusts at the turn of the sixteenth and seventeenth centuries.

As for the English, they were temporarily shaken out of the moderation which they have studiously practised both before and since by the extraordinary lavishness of Fortune when she showered Canada upon them with one hand and Bengal, simultaneously, with the other. In 1763 it seemed 'the manifest destiny' of the British Empire to swallow up the whole of North America as well as the whole of India. Yet twenty years later Great Britain had lost the better half of one of the two subcontinents and was in imminent danger of losing the whole of the other. It is true that the verdict of History has now acquitted British statesmanship of exclusive responsibility for the break-up of the First British Empire. American historians have latterly done much to show that in the fratricidal war of 1775–83 the war-guilt was divided; and the name of Warren Hastings no longer sounds so sinister as it was made to sound a century and a half ago. Nevertheless the fact remains that the Thirteen Colonies would never have been lost to the British Crown if from 1763 to 1775 it had shown towards them the same tact and consideration as it has repeatedly shown towards Canada from 1774 onwards. Nor would Bengal have been retained— nor, *a fortiori*, enlarged into an empire embracing all India—if the predatory practices of the Company's servants in the East, from Clive and Warren Hastings downwards, during the twenty-six years following the intoxicating victory of Plassey had not been discouraged by the abortive India Bill of 1783 and the effective India Bill of 1784 and the long-drawn-out state trial of 1786–95. However sincerely Clive may have 'marvelled at' his 'own moderation,' his economy of virtue would assuredly soon have cost his countrymen the loss of an Oriental dominion which his excess of unscrupulousness had suddenly won for them, if they had not exerted themselves to improve upon Clive's moral standards under the sobering influence of their American disaster.

CHAPTER VII

Goliath and David

———

In our human military history the analogue of the biological competition between the tiny soft-furred Mammal and the massive armoured Reptile is the saga of the duel between David and Goliath; and, if we take this legendary Syriac combat as our starting point, we shall find the same drama acted and re-performed in a continuous series of matches between new-fangled and old-fashioned military techniques.

Before the fatal day on which he challenges the armies of Israel, Goliath has won such triumphant victories with his spear whose staff is like a weaver's beam and whose head weighs six hundred shekels of iron, and has found himself so completely proof against hostile weapons in his panoply of casque and corselet and target and greaves, that he can no longer conceive of any alternative armament; and he believes that in this armament he is invincible. He therefore challenges the enemy of the day to choose a champion to meet him in single combat, on the assumption that, if any champion is forthcoming, he will likewise be a spearman armed *cap-à-pie*, and in the assurance that any Israelite who has the hardihood to fight the Philistine champion with his own weapons will be an easy prey for him. So hard set is Goliath's mind in these two ideas that, when he sees David running forward to meet him with no armour on his body and nothing in his hand that catches the eye except a staff, Goliath takes umbrage, instead of taking alarm, at his adversary's apparent unpreparedness, and exclaims: 'Am I a dog, that thou comest to me with staves?' Goliath does not suspect that this youth's impertinence is not a piece of boyish folly but is, on the contrary, a carefully considered manœuvre (David having actually realized, quite as clearly as Goliath himself, that in Goliath's own accoutrements he cannot hope to be Goliath's match, and having therefore rejected, after trying on, the panoply which Saul has pressed upon him); nor does Goliath notice the sling in the hand which does not hold the staff, nor wonder what mischief may be hidden in the shepherd's bag. And so this luckless Philistine Triceratops stalks forward pompously to offer his unvisored forehead as a target for the sling-stone which is to slay him at one shot before ever his contemptible adversary comes within range of his hitherto lethal spear.

Goliath of Gath was not the first hoplite in the history of Life on Earth to court and incur this disconcerting doom; for armour far more ponderous than his had been worn by reptilian and mammalian cataphracts before ever Goliath's first human ancestor had made his appearance on the terrestrial scene.

One seductive and ultimately always fatal path [of Evolution] has been the development of protective armour. An organism can protect itself by concealment, by swiftness in flight, by effective counter-attack, by uniting for attack and defence with other individuals of its species and also by encasing itself within bony plates and spines. The last course was adopted by the ganoid fishes of the Devonian with their shining armour. Some of the great lizards of the later Mesozoic were elaborately encased. Some Tertiary mammals, especially in South America, were immense and bizarre creatures; and one wonders how long a period of evolutionary history was needed for them thus to arm themselves. Always the experiment of armour failed. Creatures adopting it tended to become unwieldy. They had to move relatively slowly. Hence they were forced to live mainly on vegetable food; and thus in general they were at a disadvantage as compared with foes living on more rapidly 'profitable' animal food. The repeated failure of protective armour shows that, even at a somewhat low evolutionary level, mind triumphed over mere matter. It is this sort of triumph which has been supremely exemplified in Man.[1]

It is ideally exemplified in the saga of David and Goliath. Yet, while this classic tale sums up for all time a philosophic truth that is also illustrated by the slowly unfolding history of human competition in armaments, it is at the same time a matter of historical fact that the individual hoplite champion of the post-Minoan interregnum—a Goliath of Gath or a Hector of Troy—did not succumb to David's sling or Philoctetes' bow but to the Myrmidons' phalanx: a veritable Leviathan in which a multitude of hoplites set shoulder to shoulder and helmet to helmet and shield to shield. While each single phalangite in the rank-and-file was a replica of Hector or Goliath in his accoutrements, he was the antithesis of the Homeric hoplite in his spirit; for the essence of the phalanx did not consist in the equipment of its component men-at-arms, but in the discipline which had transformed a barbaric rabble of individual warriors into a military formation whose orderly evolutions could accomplish ten times as much as the unco-ordinated efforts of an equal number of equally well-armed individual champions.

This new military technique, of which we already catch some anticipatory glimpses in the *Iliad*, made its indubitable entry upon the stage of history in the shape of a Spartan phalanx which marched through the rhythm of Tyrtaeus' verses to its socially disastrous military victory in the Second Messeno-Spartan War; but the triumph of the Spartan phalanx was not definitive. After driving all its 'opposite numbers' off the field,

[1] Barnes, E. W.: *Scientific Theory and Religion*, pp. 474-75.

it succumbed, in its turn, to new techniques; and it is significant that this discomfiture of the Spartan phalanx came to pass
as soon as the Spartans were tempted to 'rest on their oars' on
the strength of their victory in the Atheno-Peloponnesian War
of 431–404 B.C.—a victory which seemed to complete the military supremacy of Sparta in Hellas and so to crown the victory
which the same Spartan tactics had gained over the Messenians
more than two hundred years before. Within thirty-three years
of the Athenian débâcle of 404 B.C. the triumphant Spartan
phalanx had been ignominiously put out of court: first by an
Athenian swarm of peltasts—a host of Davids with which the
phalanx of Goliaths found itself quite unable to cope—and then
by a Theban column, a tactical innovation which improved the
phalanx, with decisive effect, by introducing an uneven distri-
bution of its depth and weight and 'drive,' and thereby capping
the old asset of discipline with the new element of surprise.
The Athenian and Theban techniques, however, were as swiftly
and surely undone by their successive triumphs as the Spartan
technique itself; for their respective victories over the Spartan
phalanx in 390 and 371 were both cancelled at one stroke in
338 B.C. by a Macedonian formation in which a highly differentiated skirmisher and phalangite had been skilfully integrated
with a heavy cavalry into a single fighting force.

If the Macedonian phalanx, with its light-armed fringe and
its cavalry arm, surpassed the Spartan phalanx as an instrument
of war in the measure of the difference in range between the
Macedonian and the Spartan conquests, then the gulf between
the two techniques was great indeed, since the Spartan phalanx
merely conquered Hellas, while the Macedonian army conquered both Hellas and the Achaemenian Empire. From the
banks of the Cephisus and the Eurotas to the banks of the
Jaxartes and the Beas, the Macedonians marched at will without meeting any opponent who was able to stand up to them.

But the most impressive testimony to the prowess of the Macedonian military machine is not the long list of the military
Powers that were successively defeated by Philip II and Alexander the Great; it is the avowal which was made, after the
event, by the victorious enemy commander of the opposing
army in a decisive battle which was fought 170 years after
Philip's crushing victory at Chaeronea.

The consul Lucius [Aemilius Paullus] had never seen a phalanx
in his life until he encountered one—for the first time—in the
Roman war with Perseus; and, when it was all over, he used
freely to confess to his friends at home that the Macedonian
phalanx was the most formidable and terrifying sight that had ever
met his eyes—and this from a soldier who had not merely witnessed, but had actually participated in, a greater number of ac-
tions than any other captain of the day.[2]

At Pydna, however, in 168 B.C. it was not Perseus' phalanx but
Paullus' legions that emerged victorious; and the eulogy of the
Macedonian formation which has just been quoted is at the
same time a funeral oration pronounced over its dead body by
the master of the Roman formation which dealt the phalanx its
death-blow. The Macedonian army of the second century B.C.
was as little able to cope with the Romans as the Athenian or
Theban or Achaemenian fighting forces of the fourth century
B.C. had been able to cope with the Macedonian army of Philip
II and Alexander the Great; and the cause of this sensational
'reversal of roles' in Macedonian military fortunes was the senile
adulation of a technique which had carried all before it through
five successive generations. A hard-won Macedonian victory
over a diminutive Athens and Thebes had been followed by an
easy Macedonian conquest of the vast Achaemenian Empire;
and thereafter the Macedonian soldiers 'rested on their oars' as
the unchallenged masters of all but the outskirts of the Habita-

[2] Polybius, Book XXIX, ch. 17.

ble World, while, beyond their western horizon, the Romans
were revolutionizing the art of war through an experience
gained from their sufferings in their tremendous struggle with
Hannibal. The immense superiority of the post-Hannibalic
Roman over the post-Alexandrine Macedonian fighting-machine
was conclusively demonstrated at their first encounter; and the
omen given by the cavalry skirmish in Illyria in 200 B.C. was
fulfilled in 197 B.C. at Cynoscephalae and was confirmed in 168
B.C. at Pydna.

The Roman legion triumphed over the Macedonian phalanx
because it carried the integration of the light infantryman with
the phalangite, which the Macedonians had begun, a long step
farther. In the Macedonian technique this integration depended
on a meticulously exact co-ordination of two arms which were
at the farthest possible extreme from one another in their equipment and their training, and which were actually still segre-
gated from one another in separate units. If this vital co-ordination between the Macedonian phalanx and the Macedonian
light infantry happened to break down on the battle-field, then
either arm, just because of its extreme specialization, was in
danger of finding itself at the mercy of a more versatile adversary. Accordingly everything depended on the precision of
military evolutions in the field; and the necessary precision was
obviously impossible to guarantee. Such natural *contretemps* as
the fog at Cynoscephalae and the broken ground at Pydna
were enough to dislocate a Macedonian army's formation with
results that were disastrous when the enemy was a fighting-
force with the efficiency of the post-Hannibalic Roman army.

This Roman efficiency was a thing of yesterday; for in the
Central Italian penumbra of the Hellenic World an old-fashioned phalanx of the pre-Macedonian, and indeed pre-Theban,
type had been seen in the field at as recent a date as the day of
Cannae, when the heavy Roman infantry, embattled in an an-

tique Spartan phalanx-formation, had been rounded up from the rear by Hannibal's Spanish and Gallic heavy cavalry, and had then been slaughtered like cattle by his African heavy infantry on either flank. But in the hard school of their repeated defeats in the Hannibalic War the Romans had taught themselves an improvement in infantry technique which transformed the Roman army, at a stroke, from the least to the most efficient fighting-force in the Hellenic World of the day by eliminating the crucial weakness of the prevailing Macedonian system. In those creative years the Romans had invented a new type of armament and a new type of formation which made it possible for any given soldier, and any given unit, to play either the light infantryman's or the hoplite's part, and to change over from the one kind of tactics to the other at a moment's notice in the face of the enemy.

The superiority of this post-Hannibalic Roman infantry technique over a Macedonian technique that had been static for more than a century before the outbreak of the Second Romano-Macedonian War in 200 B.C. is lucidly explained by the contemporary Arcadian observer Polybius:

The phalanx, with its unique and potent technique, can count, as is easily demonstrable, upon sweeping away any enemy formation that ventures to face it front to front. Its charge is irresistible . . . What, then, is the explanation of the triumph of the Romans? And what is the catch that makes the employment of the phalanx spell defeat?

The catch lies in the discrepancy between that element of indeterminability—both of situations and of *terrain*—which is inherent in War as a practical art, and the inelasticity of the phalanx, which in practice can only do itself justice in one particular situation and on one particular kind of *terrain*. Of course, if, whenever it was a question of a decisive engagement, the enemy were under compulsion to accept the situation and the *terrain* that happen to suit the phalanx, then presumably the employment of the phalanx would be an infallible talisman of victory. But if it is in fact always possible—and easily possible—for the enemy to decline battle on these terms, then the phalanx-formation ceases to be formidable.

Moreover it is admitted that the phalanx requires a *terrain* which is level and clear and innocent of any such obstacles as ditches, outcrops, ravines, crags and water-courses—any of which are quite enough to throw it out of step and to dislocate its formation. It will also be admitted on all hands that the kind of *terrain* which the phalanx requires—a *terrain* innocent of obstacles over a stretch of two thousand yards and upwards—is almost impossible to find, or is at any rate exceedingly rare; and, even supposing that it has been found, it is always possible, as we have pointed out, for the enemy to decline battle . . . [or, if he does accept battle with the phalanx on level ground, the enemy can still always secure the victory by keeping part of his own force in reserve, engaging the phalanx with the rest of his force just so far as to loosen the phalanx's formation and cause it to expose its flanks, and then throwing his reserves against the flanks or rear of the phalanx when these are no longer covered by light infantry and cavalry].[3] In short, the situations that are in favour of the phalanx can be easily evaded by the enemy, whereas the phalanx cannot evade the situations that tell against it; and, if the facts as I have stated them are true, this is manifestly an enormous handicap.

Moreover a phalanx, like any other force, has to march through all kinds of country, to encamp, to forestall the enemy in occupying key-positions, to conduct and undergo sieges, and to encounter unforeseen emergencies. All these operations—which are part and parcel of War—are apt to be influential, and are sometimes decisive, in determining the issue. And for all such operations the Macedonian military technique is clumsy, and sometimes entirely ineffective, because it does not permit the phalangite to do himself justice either in the ranks or as an individual. On the other hand the Roman military technique is effective for all these operations alike, because every Roman soldier, once under arms and on duty, is equally well adapted for dealing with every kind of *terrain* and situation and emergency; and not only so, but he is

---

[3] The passage between brackets is a précis of the corresponding passage in the original.—A.J.T.

also equally in his element, and equally master of the situation, whether he is called upon to take part in a general or in a partial engagement, or to go into action by companies, or to carry on individually. It will be seen that the Roman fighting-machine is enormously superior to its rivals in its efficiency in detail, and it is therefore only natural that the Romans should be enormously more successful than their adversaries in attaining their military objectives.

This versatility, which was the characteristic feature of the full-fledged Roman military genius, made the integration of the skirmisher with the hoplite complete; for the mobility of the one and the irresistibility of the other were now combined in the person of every legionary; and when the legion, after having been evoked by Hannibal and employed, with destructive effect, against the antiquated Macedonian array, had been perfected in the Roman anti-barbarian and civil wars by a series of great captains beginning with Marius and ending with Caesar, it had attained the greatest efficiency which was possible for infantry before the invention of firearms. At the very moment, however, when the legionary was becoming perfect after his own kind, he received the first of a long series of defeats from a pair of mounted men-at-arms with utterly different techniques—the light horse-archer and the mail-clad lancer or cataphract—who between them were eventually to drive the legionary off the field *à la débandade*. The victory of the horse-archer over the legionary at Carrhae in 53 B.C. forestalled, by five years, the classic combat of legionary against legionary in 48 B.C. at Pharsalus, a battle in which the Roman infantry technique was probably at its zenith. The omen of Carrhae was confirmed, more than four centuries later, at Adrianople, where the cataphract gave the legionary his *coup de grâce* in A.D. 378.

The disaster at Adrianople, which was the tragic end of an ascendancy that the legionary had retained—albeit with increasing difficulty—for nearly six hundred years, has been vividly described by a contemporary Roman officer who was also a Latin historian.[4]

On the eve of this catastrophe the confidence of the Roman high command in the traditional Roman military technique was still so overweening that the Emperor Valens, who had just succeeded in making contact with the Gothic host that was then ravaging the Roman territory of Thrace, insisted on administering immediate punishment to the refractory barbarians. He would not wait for the reinforcements which his nephew and colleague Gratian was bringing by forced marches from the west, though he had received dispatches announcing that Gratian's army was now on the point of joining hands with his; and he would not entertain the overtures which the Goths— disconcerted at having evoked so strong a Roman military reaction—were belatedly attempting to make to their indignant Imperial adversary. Valens gave the order for his legions to march at once upon the Gothic lager; and at first sight it seemed as though his intransigent policy were justified by its effect.

The terrifying din of [the legionaries'] clashing arms, and their aggressive drumming on their shields, so intimidated the barbarians—who were also weakened by the absence of a part of their host which was operating at a distance under the command of Alatheus and Saphrax, and had not yet had time to return, though the order was on its way to them—that they sent *parlementaires* to ask for peace.

It looked as though the legions had won their victory without having had to strike a blow; but in reality Valens' intransigence had not broken the Goths' spirit but had inspired them with the courage of despair; and the parley was a feint.

The purpose of the Gothic commander Fritigern was simply

[4] Ammianus Marcellinus: *Res Gestae*, Book XXXI, ch. 11-13.

to gain time until he could take up the Roman challenge with his whole force—including the absent corps, which consisted of the heavy cavalry—and his ruse was successful; for he managed to draw the parley out—while the Romans stood to arms, without food or water, through the heat of the day—until 'the Gothic cavalry, reappearing on the scene with Alatheus and Saphrax at its head, and stiffened by a contingent of Alani, burst upon the Roman army as a thunderbolt bursts against a mountain-range, charged at lightning speed, and swept away, in a whirlwind of slaughter, as many of the Roman troops as it managed to engage at close quarters.' The legionaries were thrown out of their formation and were herded together into so dense a mass that they had no longer any room to wield, or even draw, their swords; and in this helpless plight they suffered the fate which their own predecessors had once inflicted on the Macedonian phalangites. Having caught the legionaries at this irretrievable disadvantage, the cataphracts pressed home their attack without giving their discomfited opponents a chance to rally, until 'at length, under the weight and "drive" of the barbarian offensive, the Roman line gave way, and the legionaries—driven to the last resort in a desperate situation— took to their heels in a chaotic *sauve qui peut*.' The historian vouches for the fact that 'the Roman casualties amounted to about two-thirds of the effectives engaged' (the Emperor Valens himself was among the missing); and he expresses the opinion that, 'apart from the Battle of Cannae, there' was 'no record, in all the annals of Roman military history, of any other action in which the carnage was so great as this.'

In measuring Adrianople by Cannae, Ammianus gives proof of his historical insight, for it was the slaughter at Cannae, where the Roman infantry had been at the mercy of Hannibal's heavy cavalry, that had stimulated the Roman military genius into transforming a clumsy phalanx on the old-fashioned Spar-

tan model into the mobile legion which had been victorious
first at Zama and then at Cynoscephalae and Pydna. In the year
of Adrianople, however, the lesson of Cannae was nearly six
hundred years old; and during those six centuries the Roman
legionaries had 'rested on their oars,' like the Macedonian phalangites before them, until they allowed themselves to be overtaken and ridden down by an Oriental heavy cavalry which
was a more formidable engine of war than Hannibal's European
squadrons, and which could not be coped with effectively without some fresh innovation in infantry technique. The effective
innovation was discovered in the end, but not for a thousand
years, and then not by Roman wits. Though the Romans had
received repeated warnings of the legionary's inferiority to
Oriental cavalry—in Crassus' disaster of 55 B.C. and Valerian's
of A.D. 260 and Julian's of A.D. 363—they had not been stimulated to make any fresh creative advance in infantry technique.
They had left the legion, unreformed, to its fate; and, when
'the knock-out blow' was duly delivered in the fulness of time
in A.D. 378 at Adrianople, they could think of no more original
remedy than to discard the defeated legionary outright and to
take over the victorious cataphract at second-hand. Gratian's
colleague and successor, Theodosius, rewarded the barbarian
horsemen for having annihilated the Roman infantry by hiring
them to fill the vacant place; and, even when the Imperial Government had paid the inevitable price for the brief respite that
was purchased by this short-sighted policy, and had seen the
mercenary barbarian troopers partition all its western provinces into barbarian 'successor-states,' the new native army,
which saved the Greek and Oriental provinces, at the eleventh
hour, from going the same way, was armed and mounted on
the barbarian pattern.

The ignominy of the legionary's end is accentuated by the
strange fact that the cataphract who rode him down on the

plains of Thrace in A.D. 378 was himself a degenerate. The Parthian cavalryman who had forced Crassus' legions to capitulate at Carrhae in 53 B.C. had been a horse-archer, like his native Nomad prototype; the Sarmatian and Gothic cataphracts who annihilated Valens' legions at Adrianople were mere lancers who won their victory by the crude and clumsy method of charging home, in substitution for the refined technique of overwhelming their enemy—in the manner of the Suren's horse-archers at Carrhae in 53 B.C.—with a ceaseless discharge of arrows supplied by a never-failing camel commissariat. Carrhae 'ought to have revolutionized the World's warfare; but in fact it produced little effect, for Surenas was put to death next year and his organization broken up.' The future lay not with the light horse-archer but with the cataphract, who had been represented at Carrhae in the Parthian ranks without making any notable contribution to the brilliant victory of his unarmoured comrade. And the cataphract had no sooner put on the Assyrian infantryman's armour than he had begun to discard the Nomad's bow for the hoplite's lance. The rudimentary Assyrian cataphract still remained a horse-archer; and a force of a thousand Sakas who fought for the last of the Achaemenidae at Gaugamela in 331 B.C. are described as still being equipped with bows though the horses as well as the men were armoured. When they went into action, however, these Saka demi-cataphracts did not shoot; they charged. And the Parthian full-blown cataphract who is portrayed in the *graffito* at Dura does not even carry a bow in addition to his lance. Notwithstanding the success of the light horse-archer against Crassus at Carrhae, the failure of the charging cataphract against Ventidius in the next round of this Romano-Parthian trial of strength, and the renewed success of the light horse-archer against Mark Antony, the Parthians opted for the cataphract; and the Arsacids' example was followed by their successors the Sasanidae. It is

true that Belisarius' sixth-century Roman cataphracts, as Procopius describes them, were horse-archers of the Assyrian kind;
but in general it was the armoured lancer, and not the armoured
horse-archer, who kept the saddle for the next twelve hundred
years after the light horse-archer's victory at Carrhae; and
there is an extraordinary uniformity in this lancer's accoutrements over a Time-span of more than a millennium and across
the length and breadth of Europe and Asia. His identity is un-
mistakable, whether the portrait in which he presents himself
to us happens to be in some fresco, dating from the first century of the Christian Era, in a Crimean tomb; or on the third-
and fourth- and fifth- and sixth-century bas-reliefs of Sasanian
kings in Fars; or in the clay figurines of those Far Eastern men-
at-arms who were the fighting-force of the T'ang Dynasty
(*imperabant* A.D. 618–907); or in the eleventh-century tapestry
at Bayeux which depicts the defeat of the antiquated English
foot-soldiers of the day by King William the Conqueror's Norman knights.

If this longevity and ubiquity of the cataphract are astonishing, it is also noteworthy that he only becomes ubiquitous in
a degenerate form; and, since sheer material range and scale are
apt to be symptoms of decay, we shall not be surprised when
we read the next chapter in the cataphract's history. The story
may be told, again, in the words of a contemporary who in this
case was also an eye-witness.

I was in the army of the Under-Secretary when he went forth
to meet the Tatars on the western side of the City of Peace
[Baghdad], on the occasion of its supreme disaster in the year
A.H. 656 [which began on the 8th January, A.D. 1258]. We met
at Nahr Bashīr, one of the dependencies of Dujayl; and there
would ride forth from amongst us to offer single combat a knight
fully accoutred and mounted on an Arab horse, so that it was as
though he and his steed together were [solid as] some great

mountain. Then there would come forth to meet him from the Mongols a horseman mounted on a horse like a donkey, and having in his hand a spear like a spindle, wearing neither robe nor armour, so that all who saw him were moved to laughter. Yet ere the day was done the victory was theirs, and they inflicted on us a great defeat, which was the Key of Evil, and thereafter there befell us what befell us.[5]

Thus the legendary encounter between Goliath and David at the dawn of Syriac history repeats itself at night-fall, perhaps twenty-three centuries later, as an attested historical fact; and, though on this occasion the giant and the pygmy played their parts on horseback instead of on foot, the outcome was the same.

The invincible Tatar qāzāq who overcame the 'Irāqī cataphract and sacked Baghdad and starved the 'Abbasid Caliph to death in his treasury and gave the *coup de grâce* to a Caliphate which had been a resumption of the Achaemenian Empire and a reintegration of the Syriac universal state, was a light horsearcher of the genuine and persistent Nomadic type which had made itself known, and dreaded, in South-Western Asia for the first time through the Cimmerian and Scyth eruption at the turn of the eighth and seventh centuries B.C. In the heart of the Steppe, from which the Tatars were erupting in their turn in the thirteenth century of the Christian Era, the ancient Nomad military technique had lived on to assert its superiority now, at the end of the chapter, over the armour-plated travesty of itself which was what the imitative sedentary societies had made of it in the course of some two thousand years of brief inventiveness and long stagnation. But if David-on-horseback duly discomfited Goliath-on-horseback at this historic moment, the

---

[5] Falak-ad-Dīn Muhammad b. Aydīmir, quoted at first hand by Ibn-at-Tiqtaqā in *Kitāb-al-Fakhrī*. This translation is taken from Browne, E. G.: *A Literary History of Persia*, vol. ii, p. 462.

sequel to their encounter in this repetition of the story was also
faithful to the original. We have seen that the mailed champion
on foot who was laid low by David's sling-stone was super-
seded thereafter not by David himself but by a phalanx of
Goliaths in which each phalangite was equipped with Goliath's
accoutrements but was taught to use them to better effect by
fighting in a disciplined formation instead of indulging in the
primitive sport of single combat. And now, in the Cavalry Age,
discipline won its victory over individualism once more. For
Hulāgū Khan's Mongol light horse who had overcome the
'Abbasid Caliph's knights under the walls of Baghdad in A.D.
1258 were subsequently defeated again and again—in A.D. 1260
and 1281 and 1299–1300 and 1303—whenever they swam the
Euphrates and tried conclusions with the Mamlūk masters of
Syria and Egypt under whose aegis a new series of 'Abbasid
Caliphs had found asylum. In their accoutrements the Mamlūks
were neither better nor worse equipped than their fellow Muslim knights who had been overthrown so ignominiously, a few
years before, at Nahr Bashīr; but in their tactics the Mamlūks
were true to their name and status in obeying discipline; and
this discipline gave them the mastery over Mongol sharp-shooter
and Frankish knight-errant.

Having now watched Goliath and David fight first on foot
and then on horseback,[6] we cannot leave the amphitheatre with-

[6] As a curiosity of history, the following passage, written in 1938, which
appears in the text of the original work may be reproduced here in a
footnote: [A Study of History, vol. iv, p. 463]

In the year 1938 it was again already certain that the technique which
had won the war of 1914–18 would not be the last link in the chain—if
Mankind were so perverse as to go on cultivating the Art of War after
it had attained a degree of deadliness at which any further indulgence in
belligerency seemed likely to bring with it the total destruction of Society. In another war in the West the 'post-war' British Navy and the
'post-war' French system of semi-subterranean frontier fortifications
might well prove to be nothing but mill-stones round the necks of the

out waiting to see the arena transformed into a *naumachia* for our pair of gladiators to repeat their duel afloat. We may aptly conclude our survey of the destruction which is invited by any idolization of an ephemeral technique with an illustration that is offered by one of the curiosities of naval history. When the Romans took to the sea in the course of the First Romano-Punic War (*gerebatur* 264–241 B.C.), they had to face a Carthaginian navy which was heir to all the refinements that had been introduced successively into the art of naval warfare in the Mediterranean during the two centuries that had elapsed since the generation of Themistocles. According to the story— whether this be authentic fact or the 'philosophic truth' of legend—the Roman landlubbers nonplussed the Carthaginian masters of the naval art by cancelling two centuries of naval progress at a stroke and reducing naval warfare once again to that primitive kind of land-warfare-on-shipboard which it had been at the beginning of all things. Incapable of meeting the Carthaginians on equal terms, and ruminating regretfully upon their own conspicuous ascendancy on shore, the Romans are said to have invented a gangway, slung from a mast and fitted

---

winners of what would then be remembered by Posterity, not as 'the war to end War,' but merely as the event of 1914–18 in a military competition which the lacerated competitors had failed to bring to a timely end. In another war the French fortifications might be overleapt, and the British Grand Fleet sunk in harbour, by enemy aircraft laden with all the destructive contrivances of the twentieth-century Western chemists. 'The next war,' if it ever came to wipe 'the Great Society' out of existence, might well be won—if the notion of 'victory' then still retained any meaning—by a 'post-war' professional force whose strength would lie, not in numbers, but in a discipline and training which would enable these twentieth-century Janissaries to profit to the full from an unrivalled command over an armoury of new-fangled weapons. A gang of such militarized mechanics might conquer by the same arts and virtues as the grenadiers of Frederick the Great and the musketeers of Selīm I; and if the victorious war-band of Strakers-at-arms were the German *Reichswehr*, then the wheel of European military history would have come round full circle.

with a grappling-iron, by means of which they literally came to grips with the Carthaginian warships. By this shockingly un-professional innovation in technique they seized the tactical initiative, inhibited their astonished and indignant opponents from employing their traditional tactics of manœuvring and ramming, and forcibly substituted the tactics of grappling and boarding, with decisive effects upon the fortunes of the war.

If there is any truth in this story, it brings out the connection between breakdown and idolatry very clearly; for in this in-stance we see an intrinsically superior technique which has been idolized by its adepts being defeated by an intrinsically inferior technique which has no point in its favour except that it has not yet had time to be idolized, because it is an innova-tion; and this strange spectacle suggests very forcibly that it is the act of idolization that does the mischief, and not any in-trinsic quality in the object.

CHAPTER VIII

The Price of Progress in Military Technique

Militarism has been by far the commonest cause of the breakdowns of civilizations during the four or five millennia which
have witnessed the score or so of breakdowns that are on record up to the present date. Militarism breaks a civilization
down by causing the local states into which the society is ar-
ticulated to collide with one another in destructive internecine
conflicts. In this suicidal process, the entire social fabric becomes fuel to feed the devouring flame in the brazen bosom of
Molech. The single art of war makes progress at the expense
of all the arts of peace; and, before this deadly ritual has completed the destruction of its votaries, they may have become
so expert in the use of their implements of slaughter that, if
they happen for a moment to pause in their orgy of mutual
destruction and to turn their weapons for a season against the
breasts of strangers, they are apt to carry all before them.

A case in point is the latter-day expansion of Hellenism to
India and to Britain between the fourth century B.C. and the
first century of the Christian Era; for the roads which this expansion followed had been opened by Macedonian and by Roman arms, and those arms had been wrought up to an irresistible efficiency in the long-drawn-out internecine warfare between the Great Powers of the Hellenic World in which
Athens failed to establish her hegemony and Rome succeeded

in delivering 'the knock-out blow.' Thus, in Hellenic history, Militarism was at least partly responsible for the latter-day expansion of the Hellenic World as well as for the disintegration of the Hellenic Society with which this expansion was contemporaneous.

An example of technique improving while a civilization declines is afforded by the contrast between the Upper Palaeolithic Age in Europe and the Lower Neolithic, which is its immediate successor in the technological series. The Upper Palaeolithic Society remained content with implements of rough workmanship, but it developed a fine aesthetic sense, and it did not neglect to discover certain simple means of giving its sense a pictorial expression. The deft and vivid charcoal sketches of animals, which survive on the walls of Palaeolithic Man's cave-dwellings, where they have been discovered by our modern archaeologists, excite our astonishment and admiration. The Lower Neolithic Society took infinite pains to equip itself with finely ground tools, and possibly turned these tools to account by using them as weapons in a struggle for existence with Palaeolithic Man in which *Homo Pictor* went down and left *Homo Faber* master of the field. In any case, the Palaeolithic Society vanished away and the Neolithic Society reigned in its stead; and this change, which inaugurates a striking improvement in terms of technique, is distinctly a set-back in terms of Civilization. For the art of Upper Paleolithic Man died out with him; and if Lower Neolithic Man had any glimmering of aesthetic sense at all, at any rate he has given no material expression to it.

Another example of an improvement in technique being coincident with a set-back in Civilization is to be found in the interregnum in which the Minoan Civilization went into dissolution. The Minoan Society had remained in the Bronze Age from beginning to end of its history. The latest and most barbarous swarm of Continental European barbarians who descended upon the derelict domain of the Minoan Society in the post-Minoan Völkerwanderung came armed with weapons of iron instead of bronze; and in their victorious onslaught upon the epigoni of the Minoan Civilization they doubtless profited from their acquaintance with the more potent metal. Yet this victory of the iron-sworded 'Dorians' over the bronze-sworded Minoans was a victory of Barbarism over Civilization. For an iron sword—or, for that matter, a steel tank or submarine or bombing-plane or any other killing-machine of our latter-day Machine Age—may be a talisman of victory without being a talisman of culture. When the 'Dorians' adopted weapons of iron instead of weapons of bronze, they did not cease to be barbarians. And there is no reason for crediting these barbarians even with the technical achievement of discovering a new and better material for metallurgy. The 'Dorian' iron was probably no 'Dorian' original discovery, but simply a 'Dorian' loan which a geographical accident had put these barbarians in the way of making by mimesis from the skilled artificers of a neighbouring region. In this encounter between the 'Dorians' and the Minoans, the technological criterion of progress in Civilization is confuted by a *reductio ad absurdum;* for by the technological criterion we are constrained to declare that the nadir of the post-Minoan interregnum witnessed an advance in the culture of the Aegean area; that this advance was more significant than any which had been achieved in the whole history of the Minoan Civilization; and that the advance was brought about by the invading bands of iron-sworded 'Dorians' at the moment when they were using their iron weapons to deal the bronze-sworded Minoan culture its death-blow.

This example from the history of the Old World has a parallel in the history of the New World which is remarkably exact.

The establishment of Mayan and Toltec chronology fixes, within relatively narrow limits, the beginning of the metal age in Central America and Mexico. No specimen of metal, not even a copper stain, was observed during excavations at Copan, Quirigua and other Mayan cities of the First Empire. Las Quebradas in Guatemala was actually built upon a placer mine; yet, in the sluicing operations which have almost destroyed the site, no specimen of worked gold has been found. Nor are any ornaments of metal, such as gorgets and bells, pictured on the early monuments. We therefore conclude that the metal age did not begin till after 600 A.D.; yet by 1200 A.D. metal-work was highly developed in gold, silver, copper and various alloys. Many specimens found at Chichen Itza in Northern Yucatan are of Costa Rican and Colombian origin, and the technique of metal-working is the same from Southern Colombia to Central Mexico. The art was apparently introduced from South America about A.D. 1000 and underwent a rapid growth in the five hundred years before the Spanish conquest.[1]

It will be seen that this illustration of our thesis from Central America and the preceding illustration from the Aegean throw some light upon one another. Just as in the Old World the Minoan Society performed its achievements and lived out its life without ever transcending the Bronze Age, so in the New World the Mayan Society rose and fell without ever passing out of the Stone Age into an age of metal. In Central America, the introduction of the metallurgical technique was reserved for two civilizations, both related to the Mayan, which can neither of them compare with the antecedent civilization in respect of the general level of their cultural attainments. And, here again, the technological advance was synchronous with a cultural interregnum.

If it be a *reductio ad absurdum* of the technological criterion to claim that the second-rate civilizations which were affiliated to the Mayan Civilization or the barbarian invaders of the

[1] *The Encyclopaedia Britannica:* Thirteenth Edition, vol. 1, p. 195.

Aegean World in the post-Minoan and pre-Hellenic interregnum were apostles of Civilization in virtue of their prowess in technique, it is amusing to find an equally extravagant claim being submitted by the last of the great Hellenic historians on behalf of the post-Hellenic interregnum on a similar technological ground.

Procopius of Caesarea wrote a history of the wars of the Roman Emperor Justinian (*imperabat* A.D. 527–65); and these wars were actually the death of the ancient Hellenic Society. In obstinately striving to realize his misguided ambition of restoring the territorial integrity of the Empire, Justinian brought financial ruin upon the Oriental provinces, depopulation upon the Balkan provinces, and devastation upon Italy; and even at that price he failed to achieve his 'single-track' aim; for in extirpating the Vandals in Africa he was clearing the way for the Moors to take their place, and in extirpating the Ostrogoths in Italy he was creating a vacuum which was to be filled, within three years of his own death, by the far more barbarous Lombards. The century which followed the wars of Justinian was actually the nadir of the post-Hellenic interregnum. This was the tragedy of the generation of Procopius, as posterity can see it in retrospect; and indeed it was painfully apparent at the time, and was widely recognized by Procopius' own contemporaries, that—however far off or near at hand the end of Hellenism might be—Hellenic history had long passed its zenith. Yet in writing the preface to his narrative of the fatal events which had just dealt Hellenism its death-blow before he took up his pen, the eminent historian goes out of his way to break a lance in a battle of his own seeking between the Moderns and the Ancients; and he awards the palm to the Moderns on the score of their technical superiority in the art of war.

To an unprejudiced mind it will be evident that the events of these wars are at least as striking and imposing as any in history.

They have been responsible for occurrences of a more extraordinary character than any of which a record survives, except (possibly) from the point of view of a reader who insists upon giving the palm to Antiquity and refuses to be impressed by anything in the contemporary world. The first example that occurs to my mind is the affectation of alluding to modern troops as 'archers' and reserving such appellations as 'hand-to-hand combatants' or 'men-at-arms' for the warriors of Antiquity, in the confident assumption that in our day these military qualities are extinct. Such assumptions merely betray a superficiality and an utter lack of experience in those who make them. It has never crossed their minds that the archers in Homer, whose arm is cast up against them as an opprobrious epithet, had no horse-flesh between their knees, no lance in hand, and no shield or body-armour to cover them. They went into action on foot and were compelled to take cover, either by posting themselves behind the shield of a comrade or by 'leaning against a tombstone'—a position which precluded them equally from extricating themselves in defeat and from pursuing a retreating enemy, and, above all, from fighting in the open. Hence their reputation for playing an underhand part in the game of war; while, apart from that, they took so little pains with their technique that, in shooting, they only drew the bow-string to the breast, with the natural result that the missile was spent and ineffective by the time when it reached its target. This was undoubtedly the level at which archery stood in earlier times. By contrast, modern archers go into action equipped with cuirasses and knee-boots and with their quiver on their right side and their sword on the other, while some troopers have a lance slung over their shoulders and a small handleless shield of just sufficient diameter to cover the face and neck. Being admirable horsemen, they are trained to bend their bow without effort to either flank when going at full gallop, and to hit a pursuing enemy in their rear as well as a retreating enemy to their front. They draw the bow-string to the face, to the level (approximately) of the right ear, which imparts such force to the missile that its impact is invariably fatal and that neither shield nor cuirass can resist its momentum. Some people, however, who choose to ignore the existence of these troops, persist in an open-mouthed adulation of Antiquity and refuse to admit the superiority of modern inventions. Misconceptions of this kind are, of course, powerless to rob the late wars of their superlative interest and importance.

Procopius' argument is an *extravaganza* which refutes itself; and the only comment that it seems necessary to make is that the cataphract, whom Procopius presents to his readers as the *chef d'œuvre* of Greek and Roman military technique—the most efficient type of fighting-man that had ever been thrown up in the Hellenic World during the long span of time between the Homeric Age and the author's own day—was actually no more an original creation of the Greek or the Roman military genius than iron was a discovery of the 'Dorians.' This horse-archer—armed *cap-à-pie* and formidable by reason of his personal prowess in riding and shooting—was utterly alien from the genuine Greek and Roman military tradition, which had relegated its cavalry to a subordinate role and had put its trust in an infantry whose strength lay in the corporate cohesion and discipline of the regiment far more than in the equipment or *expertise* of the individual soldier. In the Roman army, the cataphract was a recent innovation—an arm which had not been adopted more than a couple of centuries before Procopius' own day—and, if this arm had come to be the mainstay of Roman military power within that relatively short period of time, this revolution in military technique bears witness to the historic Roman infantry's rapid and lamentable decay. In fact, in the Roman army of Procopius' day the cataphract filled a vacuum which had been of the cataphract's own making; for the previously invincible Roman infantryman had first met his match, and finally acknowledged his superior, in the cataphract whom he encountered on the Mesopotamian plains in the armies of the Arsacidae and the Sasanidae, and on the Danubian plains in the war-bands of the Sarmatians and the

Goths. The military lessons of a long trial of strength between the legionary and the cataphract, which had begun with Crassus' disaster at Carrhae in 53 B.C. and had culminated in Valens' disaster at Adrianople in A.D. 378, had ultimately led the Roman authorities to discard the historic Roman infantryman—through whose sword and trenching-tool Dea Roma had originally won her Empire—and to adopt the exotic but triumphant Oriental cataphract in the legionary's stead.

In his eulogy of the cataphract, Procopius is thus really doing just the opposite of what he supposes and intends. Instead of celebrating an improvement of the Greek and Roman military technique, he is pronouncing its funeral oration. Yet, although Procopius has chosen an unfortunate illustration of the point that he is seeking to make, his general contention that there has been a progressive improvement in Hellenic technique remains broadly true within the field of military technique to which he confines his argument. In surveying this field of Greek and Roman social history, let us rule out of account the spurious epilogue represented by the cataphract and confine our survey to the thousand years which began with the invention of the Spartan phalanx in the Second Messeno-Spartan War in the latter part of the seventh century B.C. and which ended with the final discomfiture and discrediting of the Roman legion at the Battle of Adrianople in A.D. 378. The development of the genuinely Hellenic military technique can be traced, without any break in continuity, throughout these thousand years; and in tracing it we shall find that an arrest or a set-back in the Hellenic Civilization invariably accompanied an improvement in the Hellenic art of war.

To begin with, as we have seen already, the invention of the Spartan phalanx, which is the first signal improvement of which we have a record, was an outcome of the same events that brought the growth of the Spartan version of the Hellenic Civilization to a premature halt.

The next signal improvement was the differentiation of the Hellenic infantryman into two extreme types: the Macedonian phalangite and the Athenian peltast. The Macedonian phalanx, armed with long two-handed pikes in place of short one-handed stabbing-spears, was more formidable in its impact than its Spartan precursor; but it was also more unwieldy in its manœuvres and more at the enemy's mercy if once it lost its formation; and therefore it could not safely go into action unless its flanks were guarded by peltasts: a new type of light infantry who were taken out of the ranks and trained to fight as skirmishers. In collaboration, the Macedonian phalangite and the Athenian peltast were a far more effective type of infantry than the old undifferentiated phalangite on the Spartan model; and this second improvement in the Hellenic military technique was the outcome of a century of internecine warfare in the Hellenic World—the century running from the outbreak of the Atheno-Peloponnesian War in 431 B.C. to the Macedonian victory at Chaeronea in 338—which saw the Hellenic Civilization break down and go into disintegration.

The next signal improvement in the Hellenic military technique was made by the Romans, when they succeeded in combining the advantages and avoiding the defects of both peltast and phalangite in the tactics and equipment of the legionary. The legionary was armed with a couple of throwing-spears and a stabbing-sword, and the legion went into action in open order in two waves, with a third wave—armed and ordered in the old-fashioned phalanx-style—in reserve. This third improvement in the Hellenic military technique was the outcome of a fresh bout of internecine warfare—beginning with the outbreak of the Hannibalic War in 218 B. C. and closing with the end of the Third Romano-Macedonian War in 168—in which the Romans delivered a 'knock-out blow' to every other Great Power in the Hellenic World of that age.

The fourth and last improvement was the perfection of the legion: a process, begun by Marius and completed by Caesar, which was the outcome of a century of Roman revolutions and civil wars. The Roman legionary was probably at his best in the army which fought for Caesar at Pharsalus in 48 B.C.—five years after the legions which had fought for Crassus at Carrhae in 53 B.C. had met their match in the Parthian cataphracts. Thus the generation of Caesar and Crassus saw the Greek and Roman military technique both attain and pass its zenith. And the same generation saw the Hellenic Civilization enter upon the penultimate stage in its decline and fall. For that century of Roman revolutions and civil wars which had begun in 133 B.C. with the tribunate of Tiberius Gracchus had been the climax of the Hellenic 'Time of Troubles'; and it was Caesar's mission to bring that 'Time of Troubles' to a close by inaugurating the universal state which Augustus eventually established after the Battle of Actium.

In this history of the successive improvements in the Hellenic art of war, we have a clear case in which it is not the growth of a civilization, but its arrest and breakdown and disintegration, that goes hand in hand with the improvements in its military technique; and the histories of the Babylonic and Sinic Civilizations offer us equally good illustrations of the same phenomenon. Both in the Babylonic 'Time of Troubles,' when the Babylonic Society was tearing itself to pieces in the frenzy of Assyrian militarism, and likewise in the Sinic 'Time of Troubles,' when the military Power of Ts'in was delivering 'knock-out blows' to the other contending states of the Sinic World, conspicuous improvements in military technique were accomplished. In both cases, for example, the old-fashioned use of the war-horse as a draught-animal to draw a chariot was discarded in favour of its more effective use as a mount for a cavalryman. Perhaps we may infer from the foregoing survey that an improvement in military technique is usually, if not invariably, the symptom of a decline in Civilization.

An Englishman of the generation that has lived through the General War of 1914–18 may remind himself, in this connection, of an incident which struck him, at the time, as painfully symbolic. As the War, in its ever-increasing intensity, made wider and wider demands upon the lives of the belligerent nations—like some great river that has burst its bounds in flood and is engulfing field after field and sweeping away village after village—a moment came in England when the offices of the Board of Education in Whitehall were commandeered for the use of a new department of the War Office which had been improvised in order to make an intensive study of trench warfare. The ejected Board of Education found asylum in the Victoria and Albert Museum, where it survived on sufferance as though it had been some curious relic of a vanished past. And thus, for several years before the Armistice of the 11th November, 1918, an education for slaughter was being promoted, in the heart of our Western World, within the walls of a public building which had been erected in order to assist in promoting an education for life. As the writer of this volume was walking down Whitehall one day in the spring of that year 1918, he found himself repeating a passage from the Gospel according to Saint Matthew:

When ye therefore shall see the abomination of desolation, spoken of by Daniel the Prophet, stand in the holy place, (whoso readeth, let him understand), . . . then shall be great tribulation, such as was not since the beginning of the World to this time . . . And, except those days should be shortened, there should no flesh be saved . . .

No reader can fail to understand that when the Ministry of Education of a great Western country is given over to the study of the art of war, the improvement in our Western military technique which is purchased at such a price is synonymous with the destruction of our Western Civilization.

CHAPTER IX

The Failure of the Saviour with the Sword

———

The would-be saviour of a disintegrating society is necessarily a saviour with a sword; but a sword may be either drawn or sheathed, and the swordsman may be discovered in either of two corresponding postures. Either he may be laying about him with naked weapon in hand, like the Gods in combat with the Giants as they are depicted on the Delphic or on the Pergamene frieze, or else he may be sitting in state, with his blade out of sight in its scabbard, as a victor who has 'put all enemies under his feet.' The second of these postures is the end towards which the first is a means; and, though a David or a Hêraklês, who never rests from his labours until he dies in harness, may be a more romantic figure than a Solomon in all his glory or a Zeus in all his majesty, the labours of Hêraklês and the wars of David would be aimless exertions if the serenity of Zeus and the prosperity of Solomon were not their objectives. The sword is only wielded in the hope of being able to use it to such good purpose that it may eventually have no more work to do; but this hope is an illusion; for it is only in fairyland that swords cut Gordian knots which cannot be untied by fingers. 'All they that take the sword shall perish with the sword' is the inexorable law of real life; and the swordsman's belief in a conclusive victory is an illusion. While David may never be allowed to build the Temple, Solomon's building is built only to be burnt by Nebuchadnezzar; and,

while Hêraklês may never win his way in this life to the
heights of Olympus, Zeus plants his throne upon the formidable mountain's summit only to court the doom of being
hurled in his turn into the abyss into which his own hands
have already cast the Titans.

Why is it that a disintegrating society cannot, after all, be
saved by the sword even when the swordsman is genuinely
eager to return the weapon to its scabbard at the earliest possible moment and to keep it there—unused and unseen—for the
longest possible period of time? Is not this twofold action of
drawing and sheathing again a sign of grace which ought to
have its reward? The warrior who is willing to renounce, at
the first opportunity, the use of an instrument which he is
only able now to lay aside because he has just used it so successfully must be a victor who is also a statesman, and a statesman who is something of a sage. He must have a large measure
of saving common sense and at least a grain of the more
etherial virtue of self-control. The renunciation of War as an
instrument of policy is a resolution which promises to be as
fruitful as it is noble and wise; and, whenever it is taken with
sincerity, it always arouses high hopes.

Why are these seemingly legitimate expectations doomed to
be disappointed—as they were in the signal failure of the *Pax
Augusta* to achieve the perpetuity that was hoped for it? Is
there, then, 'no place of repentance'? Can the Triumvir who
has once perpetrated, and profited by, the proscriptions never
truly transfigure himself into a Pater Patriae? The answer to
this agonizing question has been given in an Horatian ode by
an English poet upon the return of a Western Caesar from a
victorious campaign in which the victor seemed at last to have
triumphantly completed his military task. A poem which pur-
ports to be a paean in honour of a particular victory sounds the
knell of all Militarism in its last two stanzas:

But thou, the War's and Fortune's son,
March indefatigably on;
  And, for the last effect,
  Still keep the sword erect.

Besides the force it has to fright
The spirits of the shady night,
  The same arts that did gain
  A power, must it maintain.[1]

This classically phrased verdict upon the career of the earliest would-be saviour with the sword in the modern history of our Western Civilization has a sting in its tail which pricks with a still sharper point in the nineteenth-century *mot* that 'the one thing which you cannot do with bayonets is to sit on them.' An instrument that has once been used to destroy life cannot then be used to preserve life at the user's convenience. The function of weapons is to kill; and a ruler who has not scrupled to 'wade through slaughter to a throne' will find—if he tries to maintain his power thereafter without further recourse to the grim arts which have gained it—that sooner or later he will be confronted with a choice between letting the power slip through his fingers or else renewing his lease of it by means of another bout of bloodshed. The man of violence cannot both genuinely repent of his violence and permanently profit by it. The law of *karma* is not evaded so easily as that. The saviour with the sword may perhaps build a house upon the sand but never the house upon a rock. And he will not be able to build for Eternity vicariously by the expedient of a division of labour between a blood-guilty David and an innocent Solomon; for the stones with which Solomon builds will have been of David's hewing; and the veto pronounced against the father —'Thou shalt not build an house for my name because thou hast

[1] Andrew Marvell: *An Horatian Ode upon Cromwell's Return from Ireland.*

been a man of war and hast shed blood'—spells doom for a house built by the son on the father's behalf.

This ultimate failure of all attempts to win salvation with the sword is not only proclaimed in poetry and myth and legend; it is also demonstrated in history; for 'the iniquity of the fathers' who have had recourse to the sword is visited 'upon the children unto the third and fourth generation.' In our own day the descendants of the Protestant English military colonists whom Cromwell planted in Ireland to hold a conquered Catholic country down have been evicted from their ancestors' ill-gotten estates by the very weapons of violence and injustice to which they owed their cursed heritage; and, in 1937, the wealth of a British community of business men in a treaty-port and settlement at Shanghai which had been founded on the iniquity of 'the Opium War' of A.D. 1840–42 was being destroyed by Japanese and Chinese hands which had been schooled in Militarism by the example of past British success in temporarily transmuting military violence into commercial profit. Nor are these two judgements of History exceptional. The classic saviours with the sword have been the captains and the princes who have striven to found or have succeeded in founding or have succeeded in preserving or have striven to preserve the universal states into which the disintegrating civilizations pass when they have lived through their 'Times of Troubles' to the bitter end; and, although the passage from 'Time of Troubles' to universal state is apt to bring with it so great an immediate relief for the tormented children of a disintegrating society that they sometimes show their gratitude to the successful founder of a universal state by worshipping him as a god, we shall find, when we come to study these universal states more closely, that they are at best ephemeral, and that if, by a *tour de force*, they obstinately outlive their normal span they have to pay for this unnatural longevity by degenerating into social enormities which are as pernicious in their way as either the 'Times of Troubles' that precede the establishment of universal states or the interregna that follow their break-up at the normal age.

The association between the histories of universal states and the careers of would-be saviours with the sword does not merely testify in a general way to the inefficacy of force as an instrument of salvation: it enables us to survey the evidence empirically by giving us a convenient clue for sorting out the would-be saviours of this kind and marshalling them in an order in which it becomes possible to pass them in review.

The first to march past will be the tragic battalion of would-be saviours with the sword who have slashed—with blades as futile as the Danaids' sieves—at the welling wars of a 'Time of Troubles.'

In the Hellenic 'Time of Troubles' (*circa* 431–31 B.C.) we can perceive, in the first generation, the gallant figure of a Lacedaemonian Brasidas giving his life to liberate the Greek city-states in Chalcidicê from an Athenian yoke—only to have his work undone within less than half a century by other Lacedaemonian hands which were to open the way for a Philip of Macedon to place a heavier yoke upon the neck of every state in Hellas save Sparta herself. At Brasidas' heels stalks the sinister figure of his countryman and contemporary, Lysander, who successfully liberated the Greek city-states along the Asiatic shores of the Aegean and gave the Athenian 'thalassocracy' its *coup de grâce*—only to bring upon the former subjects of Athens the chastisement of Lacedaemonian scorpions in place of Attic whips and to set his own country's feet upon a path that was to lead her, in thirty-three years, from Aegospotami to Leuctra. Thereafter each successive generation adds some figure to our parade. We see a Theban Epaminondas liberating the Arcadians and Messenians and punishing Sparta

as Lysander had punished Athens—only to stimulate the Pho-
cians to inflict the same punishment on Thebes herself. We see
a Macedonian Philip ridding Hellas of the Phocian scourge and
being hailed as 'friend, benefactor, and saviour' by the Thebans and Thessalians who had been the principal sufferers from
it—only to extinguish the freedom of these two Hellenic peoples
that once had been so naïve as to 'think the whole world of
him.' And we see an Alexander seeking to reconcile the Hellenes to a Macedonian hegemony by leading them on the quest
of making a common prize of the entire Achaemenian Empire
—only to lose for Macedon the hegemony which his father had
won for her, and to feed the flames of Hellenic civil war by
pouring into the rival war-chests of his own successors a treasure which the Achaemenidae had been accumulating for two
centuries.

A parallel and contemporary procession of unsuccessful
saviours with the sword can be observed in that other half of
the Hellenic World which lay to the west of the Adriatic. We
have only to recite the catalogue of their names—Dionysius the
First and Dionysius the Second, Agathoclês and Hiero and
Hieronymus—in order to perceive that the failure of each of
these dictators in turn is proclaimed in the bare fact of his
needing a successor to grapple with the same task all over again.
The problem of saving Hellenism in the West by establishing
an *union sacrée* which would be strong enough to resist the
dual pressure of Syriac rivals from Africa and barbarian inter-
lopers from Italy remained unsolved until the fertile seed-bed
of Hellenic culture in Sicily was devastated by being turned
into the arena of a struggle for oecumenical dominion between
Carthage and Rome.

In the Orthodox Christian World the same battalion of
would-be saviours is represented by figures who are more sym-
pathetic without being more effective. In the main body of

Orthodox Christendom we see Alexius Comnenus (*imperabat* A.D. 1081–1118) snatching a prostrate East Roman Empire out of the jaws of Normans and Saljūqs with all the intrepidity of a David rescuing his lamb from the lion and the bear. And a century later we see a Theodore Lascaris refusing to despair of the republic after the unprecedented and overwhelming catastrophe of A.D. 1204, and turning at bay, behind the walls of Nicaea, against the Frankish conquerors of the holy city of Constantine. But all this Byzantine heroism was in vain. For in the tragic history of the East Roman Empire the French Goliath who came prowling on the Fourth Crusade did not, after all, share the fate of the Norman bear and the Saljūq lion; and the eventual recapture of Constantinople by Michael Palaeologus, which seemed at the moment to have crowned Theodore Lascaris' work with a posthumous success, proved in the sequel only to have sealed the East Roman Empire's doom by showing the 'Osmanlis the way from the Asiatic to the European side of the Black Sea Straits. In the history of the Russian offshoot of the Orthodox Christian Society we may discern counterparts of an Alexius Comnenus and a Theodore Lascaris in Alexander Nevski (*regnabat* A.D. 1252–63) and Dmitri Donskoi (*regnabat* A.D. 1362–89), who wielded their swords for the salvation of the Russian World, during its separate 'Time of Troubles' (*circa* A.D. 1078–1478), from the simultaneous assaults of Lithuanian pagans and Teutonic Crusaders on the north-west and of Mongol Nomads on the south-east. These Russian heroes of Orthodox Christendom were happier in their generation than their Greek peers, since the fort which they held so valiantly against such heavy odds was not, in the next chapter of the story, to fall into alien hands. Yet Alexander and Dmitri were no more successful than Alexius or Theodore in fulfilling their personal task of bringing a 'Time of Troubles' to an end.

These saviours with the sword whose lot has fallen in 'Times of Troubles' are patently cast in the mould of Hêraklês without a touch of Zeus; but the next battalion that comes marching at their heels consists of half-castes between the Herculean and the Jovian type who are not dispensed from performing Hercules' labours but are also not condemned to perform them without any hope of obtaining Jove's reward. These Jovian Herculeses or Herculean Joves are the forerunners of the successful founders of universal states. They play the part of a Moses to a Joshua or an Elias to a mundane Messiah or a John the Baptist to a Christ (if the would-be saviours of a mundane society may properly be brought into comparison with the harbingers of a kingdom which is not of This World). Some of these forerunners die without passing over Jordan or obtaining more than a Pisgah-sight of the Promised Land, while there are others who succeed in forcing the passage and in momentarily planting the standard of their kingdom on the farther bank; but these audacious spirits who seek to wrest a premature success out of the hands of a reluctant Destiny are visited, for their temerity, with a punishment that is escaped by their peers who recognize, and bow to, their fate; for the universal states which they prematurely set up collapse, like houses of cards, as swiftly as they have been erected; and the jerry-builders' abortive labours only find a place in history as a foil to display the solidity of the work of successors who retrieve the disaster by rebuilding the fallen edifice in granite instead of pasteboard.

The Moses who dies in the Wilderness is represented in Hellenic history by a Marius, who showed the way for a Julius to follow in the next generation, though Marius' own hesitant and clumsy moves towards the establishment of an egalitarian dictatorship not only failed to introduce a reign of order but grievously aggravated an existing state of anarchy. In the main body of Orthodox Christendom the 'Osmanlī Bāyezīd Yilderim came within an ace of anticipating Mehmed the Conqueror's double achievement of capturing Constantinople and settling scores with Qāramān, when 'the Thunderbolt' was blasted in mid-action by the sudden and irresistible impact of a still mightier military force.

Next to this vanguard who see, but never set foot on, the Promised Land comes a second company of forerunners who momentarily subdue the monster of anarchy—but this not so decisively that he cannot raise his head or show his teeth again.

In the Hellenic World a Pompey and a Caesar divided between them the task of reforming a Roman anarchy into a Roman Peace—only to share the guilt of undoing their common work by turning their arms against each other. The rival war-lords condemned a world which it was their joint mission to save to be scarified by another bout of Roman civil war; and the victor triumphed only to be 'rejected,' like Esau, 'when he would have inherited the blessing,' and to find 'no place of repentance, though he sought it carefully with tears.' Caesar did not expiate the deaths of Pompey and Cato by his famous clemency in the hour of his apparent omnipotence. The slayer who had stayed his sword from further slaughter had nevertheless to die by the daggers of defeated adversaries whose lives he had spared; and in dying this tragic death Caesar bequeathed yet another bout of civil war as his unwilled legacy to a piteous world which he had sincerely desired to save. The sword had to take a further toll of life and happiness before the task which Caesar and Pompey had so lightly thrown to the winds was well and truly executed at last by Caesar's adopted son. Augustus did succeed, after the overthrow of the last of his adversaries, in demobilizing the swollen armies that were left on his hands on the morrow of the Battle of Actium.

In Syriac history Divus Julius has his counterpart in Cyrus, the would-be bringer of a *Pax Achaemenia* to a world that had been lacerated by a *furor Assyriacus*. It was in vain that Cyrus (as the story goes) paid heed to the sign sent from Heaven by Apollo and repented of the evil that he thought to do unto Croesus. Instead of burning his vanquished adversary alive, Cyrus took Croesus for his trusted counsellor—only (according to the Herodotean tale) to lose his life, years afterwards, through acting on bad advice which Croesus had given him in good faith. The last word on Cyrus' career was spoken by the queen of the Nomads when she promised to satisfy the Persian war-lord's insatiable appetite for blood; and Tomyris duly carried out her threat on the stricken field by filling a wine-skin with the blood of the slain and dabbling in it the lips of Cyrus' corpse. Nor was it only Cyrus himself who perished by the stroke of the weapon which he had drawn; for the death of the Achaemenid empire-builder was capped by the collapse of his imposing edifice. Cambyses played the same havoc with Cyrus' *Pax Achaemenia* as a Gaius and a Nero played with Octavian's *Pax Augusta;* and Darius had to salvage Cyrus' ruined work, as Vespasian salvaged Augustus'.

In the same Syriac World more than a thousand years later, when the Arab war-lord 'Umar brought a long interlude of Hellenic intrusion to a tardy end by emulating the Persian war-lord Cyrus' lightning-swift feats of conquest, the captor of Jerusalem showed the same clemency as the captor of Sardis—only to demonstrate once again that, for the would-be saviour with the sword, there is 'no place of repentance.' Once again a sword-built edifice collapsed as soon as the builder's sword-arm had been put out of action. After 'Umar's death his work—like Cyrus'—was first shamefully wrecked and then brilliantly salvaged—though, in the history of the Caliphate, Cambyses' and Darius' roles were both of them played, turn and turn about, by the versatile genius of a single Arab statesman. Mu'āwīyah

coldly condemned a world that had just been exhausted by the
last round of an inconclusive struggle between Rome and Persia to be further harried by an Arab civil war in order that the
astute Umayyad might filch the political heritage of the Prophet
Muhammad out of the incompetent hands of the Prophet's own
cousin and son-in-law.

There is, however, a third company in our battalion of forerunners, and this is composed of Herculeses who hand on to
successors the fruits of their own labours without ever tasting
these fruits for themselves, but also without any break or set-
back. In the Babylonic World, Nabopolassar (*imperabat* 626-
605 B.C.) spent his life in compassing the death of the Assyrian
tiger in order that Nebuchadnezzar (*imperabat* 605–562 B.C.)
might sit, unchallenged, on the throne of a Neo-Babylonian
Empire which could not stand secure until Nineveh lay in
ruins.

To the eyes of an historian of a later age, who can see the
careers of the founders of universal states in the light of a distant sequel, their Jovian figures do not stand out as being strikingly different from the Herculean figures of their predecessors. But to the eyes of a contemporary observer, who cannot
see things in perspective, there seems to be all the difference
here between failure and success. The founders of the universal
states appear at the moment to have triumphantly achieved a
success which their predecessors have striven for manfully but
in vain; and the genuineness of this success appears to be guar-
anteed not merely by the effectiveness of the founders' own
lives and deeds (however eloquently these facts may speak),
but most decisively of all by the prosperity of the founders'
successors. Solomon's glory is the most telling evidence for
David's prowess. Let us therefore now continue our survey of
saviours with the sword by passing in review these Solomons
who are born into the purple. The swords of the *porphyro-*

geniti are speciously muffled in the folds of an imperial robe; and, if ever we see them show their true colours by displaying the hidden blade, we shall always find that this act of self-betrayal has been prompted by wantonness and not enjoined by necessity. If salvation with the sword is to be 'justified of her children,' it must be now, in this Solomonian generation, or never in the whole history of the disintegrations of civilizations. So let us inspect our Solomons closely.

The reigns of these Solomons constitute those relatively happy periods of partial peace and prosperity which look like 'Golden Ages' if we confine our view to the life-spans of the universal states in which they occur, but which can be seen to be really 'Indian Summers' as soon as we extend our field of vision to include the whole life-span of the civilization in whose history the coming and going of a universal state is only one of a number of incidents in a long tale of disintegration. An empirical survey of these 'Indian Summers' will bring out two salient features of this historical phenomenon. We shall find that they display a striking uniformity of character combined with an equally striking inequality of duration.

The Hellenic 'Indian Summer' began at the accession of the Emperor Nerva in A.D. 96 and ended at the death of the Emperor Marcus in A.D. 180; and these eighty-four years amount to not much less than a quarter of the total duration of a *Pax Romana* which, in the terms of the conventional chronology which dates by public events, may be reckoned to have begun in 31 B.C., on the morrow of the Battle of Actium, and to have ended in A.D. 378, on the day of the Battle of Adrianople. In the history of the Egyptiac Society the 'Indian Summer' of 'the New Empire' lasted longer—from the accession of Thothmes I, *circa* 1545 B.C., to the death of Amenhotep III in 1376 B.C. But both these spans are surpassed in the duration of the 'Indian Summer' of 'the Middle Empire,' which was the original Egyptiac universal state; for this first Egyptiac 'Indian Summer' was almost coeval with the Twelfth Dynasty, which reigned, from first to last, *circa* 2000–1788 B.C.; and, even if we date the onset of winter from the death of Amenemhat III in 1801 B.C., the spell of sunshine covers half the total duration of a *Pax Thebana* that lasted in all for about four centuries, if its beginning is to be equated with the accession of Mentuhotep IV, *circa* 2070–2060 B.C., and its end with the eruption of the Hyksos, *circa* 1660 B.C.

These 'Indian Summers' that have lasted through successive reigns, and in at least one case for almost the whole period of a dynasty, differ notably in length from other 'Indian Summers' which are also manifestly authentic examples of the same social phenomenon, but which have not outlasted the reign of some single sovereign with whose name they are identified. In the history of the Arab Caliphate the celebrated 'Indian Summer' in the reign of Hārūn-ar-Rashīd (*imperabat* A.D. 786–809) shines out so brilliantly thanks to the depth of the darkness in which this pool of light is framed. The splendours of an 'Abbasid Caliph who was profiting by the cumulative results of the labours of a long line of Umayyad predecessors are set off on the one hand by an antecedent bout of anarchy in which Hārūn's 'Abbasid forebears had wrested the Caliphate out of the Umayyads' grasp, and on the other hand by a subsequent débâcle, in which Hārūn's 'Abassid successors fell into a humiliating bondage to their own Turkish body-guard.

In the main body of Orthodox Christendom the *Pax Ottomanica* produced its 'Indian Summer' in the reign of Suleymān the Magnificent (*imperabat* A.D. 1520–66)—an 'Osmanli prince who emulated 'in real life' the legendary glory of his Davidic namesake. Suleymān's Western contemporaries were affected like the Queen of Sheba by the vastness of this latter-day Solomon's dominions and the abundance of his wealth and the gran-

deur of his buildings; 'there was no more spirit in' them. Yet
the curse which the biblical Solomon lived to bring down on
himself was also incurred by Suleymān. 'The Lord said unto
Solomon: "Forasmuch as this is done of thee, and thou hast not
kept my covenant and my statutes which I have commanded
thee, I will surely rend the kingdom from thee and will give it
to thy servant."' Suleymān the Magnificent was the Ottoman
Pādishāh who sapped the foundations of the Ottoman social
system by making the first breach in the fundamental rule that
the Pādishāh's Slave-Household must be recruited from persons
who were infidel-born, and that Muslim freemen should be
ineligible for enlistment *ex officio religionis*. In tolerating the
enrolment of Janissaries' sons among the *'Ajem-oghlans*, Suleymān opened the flood-gates for a disastrous dilution of the
Janissary Corps; and this self-inflicted catastrophe duly rent
the kingdom from the 'Osmanlī Pādishāh and gave it to his
'human cattle' the *ra'īyeh*.

If we now turn our eyes from the main body of Orthodox
Christendom to its offshoot in Russia, we may hesitate at first
sight to recognize a counterpart of Suleymān the Magnificent
in his contemporary Ivan the Terrible (*imperabat* A.D. 1533–84).
Are a reign of terror and an 'Indian Summer' compatible? The
two atmospheres will strike us as being so sharply antipathetic
to one another that we may question the possibility of their
co-existing in a single place and time. Yet the record of Ivan
the Terrible's achievements may compel us to admit that his
reign was an 'Indian Summer' of a sort; for this was the reign
which saw the prince of Muscovy assume the style and title of
an East Roman Emperor and justify this audacity by the conquest of Qāzān and Astrakhan and the opening-up of the
White Sea and Siberia. This was assuredly an 'Indian Summer,'
albeit with thunder in the air; and this reading of Ivan the Terrible's reign is confirmed by the sequel. Before the Emperor's

death a shadow was thrown athwart the sinister sunlight of his reign by the outcome of a war for the acquisition of a seaboard on the Baltic which dragged on even longer than the war subsequently waged for the same purpose by Peter the Great, but which ended in a miserable failure that was at the opposite pole from Peter's brilliant success. And when Ivan had gone to his account the strokes of misfortune fell thick and fast upon the body politic which he left behind him. The year 1598 saw the extinction of the House of Rurik, and the years 1604–13 saw a temporary collapse of the Russian Orthodox Christian universal state from which it did not fully recover till the reign of Peter the Great.

If we now glance back at our catalogue of 'Indian Summers' that have endured for longer than a single reign, we shall observe that these too, for all their staying-power, have succumbed to the onset of winter in the end. In the Hellenic World Marcus was followed by Commodus, and Alexander Severus by 'the Thirty Tyrants.' In the Egyptiac World in the days of 'the New Empire' Amenhotep III was followed by an Amenhotep IV who has made himself notorious under his self-chosen title of Ikhnaton, while in the days of 'the Middle Empire' the long series of majestically alternating Amenemhats and Senwosrets gave way at last to a dynasty in which no fewer than thirteen ephemeral emperors successively seized and lost the Imperial Throne within the brief span of a quarter of a century.

Our survey of 'Indian Summers' has thus, it would appear, been leading us to the conclusion that the careers of the Solomons decisively refute, instead of decisively vindicating, the claim of the sword to be convertible into an instrument of salvation; for, whether an 'Indian Summer' lasts out the life of a dynasty or comes and goes within the briefer span of a single reign, we have seen that it is in any case essentially something

transitory. The glory of Solomon is a glory that fades; and, if
Solomon is a failure, then David—and David's forerunners—
have wielded their swords in vain. The truth seems to be that
a sword which has once drunk blood cannot be permanently
restrained from drinking blood again, any more than a tiger
who has once tasted human flesh can be prevented from becoming a man-eater from that time onwards. The man-eating
tiger is, no doubt, a tiger doomed to death; if he escapes the
bullet he will die of the mange. Yet, even if the tiger could
foresee his doom, he would probably be unable to subdue the
devouring appetite which his first taste of man-meat has awak-
ened in his maw; and so it is with a society that has once sought
salvation through the sword. Its leaders may repent of their
butcher's work; they may show mercy on their enemies, like
Caesar, and demobilize their armies, like Augustus; and, as they
ruefully hide the sword away, they may resolve in complete
good faith that they will never draw it again except for the
assuredly beneficent, and therefore legitimate, purpose of preserving the peace against criminals still at large within the borders of their tardily established universal state or against barbarians still recalcitrant in the outer darkness. They may clinch
this resolution with an oath and reinforce it with an exorcism;
and for a season they may appear to have successfully achieved
the pious *tour de force* of bitting and bridling Murder and har-
nessing him to the chariot of Life; yet, though their fair-
seeming *Pax Oecumenica* may stand steady on its grim foundation of buried sword-blades for thirty or a hundred or two
hundred years, Time sooner or later will bring their work to
naught.

Time is, indeed, working against these unhappy empire-
builders from the outset; for sword-blades are foundations that
never settle. Exposed or buried, these blood-stained weapons
still retain their sinister charge of *karma;* and this means that

they cannot really turn into inanimate foundation-stones, but must ever be stirring—like the dragon's-tooth seed that they are —to spring to the surface again in a fresh crop of slaying and dying gladiators. Under its serene mask of effortless supremacy the Oecumenical Peace of a universal state is fighting, all the time, a desperate losing battle against an unexorcized demon of Violence in its own bosom; and we can see this moral struggle being waged in the guise of a conflict of policies.

Can the Jovian ruler of a universal state succeed in curbing that insatiable lust for further conquests which was fatal to Cyrus? And, if he cannot resist the temptation *debellare superbos*, can he at any rate bring himself to act on the Virgilian counsel *parcere subiectis?* When we apply this pair of tests to Jovius' performance, we shall find that he seldom succeeds in living up for long to his own good resolutions.

In the history of the Hellenic universal state the founder himself set a practical example of moderation to his successors by abandoning his attempt to carry the Roman frontier to the Elbe, before he bequeathed to them his famous counsel to be content with preserving the Empire within its existing limits, without attempting to extend it. Augustus' attitude is illustrated by Strabo's account of a current controversy over the question whether the Augustan rule might allow of a British exception. And, although this particular breach of the rule was eventually committed with an apparent impunity, Trajan afterwards demonstrated the soundness of Augustus' judgement when he ventured to break the rule on the grand scale by attempting to realize Crassus' and Julius' and Antonius' dream of conquering the Parthian Empire. The price of a momentary advance from the hither bank of Euphrates to the foot of Zagros and the head of the Persian Gulf was an intolerable strain upon the Roman Empire's resources in money and men. Insurrections broke out not only in the newly conquered territories

between the conquerer's feet but also among the Jewish Diasporà in the ancient dominions of the Empire in his rear; the
clear sky of a nascent Hellenic 'Indian Summer' was momentarily overcast; and it took all the prudence and ability of
Trajan's successor Hadrian to liquidate the formidable legacy
which Trajan's sword had bequeathed to him. Hadrian
promptly evacuated all his predecessor's Transeuphratean conquests; yet he was able to restore only the territorial, and not
the political, *status quo ante bellum*. Trajan's act of aggression
made a deeper mark on Transeuphratean Syriac minds than
Hadrian's reversal of it; and we may date from this epoch the
beginning of a change of temper in the Transeuphratean tract
of the Syriac World which was fostered by Roman relapses
into a recourse to the sword until the reaction in Iran declared
itself at length in sensational fashion in the revolutionary re-
placement of an Arsacid King Log by a Sasanid King Stork,
and the consequent resumption of that militant counter-attack
against the Hellenic intruder which had succeeded in evicting
Hellenism from its footholds in Iran and 'Irāq in the second
century B.C., but had latterly been in suspense since the conclusion by Augustus, in 20 B.C., of a Romano-Parthian 'peace with
honour.' Under the auspices of the second Pādishāh of the
Sasanian line the Trajanic breach of the Augustan rule in A.D.
113–17 found its nemesis in A.D. 260 in a repetition of the disaster which had been inflicted upon Roman arms in 53 B.C. by
the Parthians.

In Egyptiac history we see the Theban sword that had been
drawn in a *Befreiungskrieg* by Amosis (*imperabat* 1580–1558
B.C.) and wielded in a *revanche* by Thothmes I (*imperabat*
1545–1514 B.C.) being deliberately sheathed by the Empress
Hatshepsut (*imperabat* 1501–1479 B.C.)—only to be wilfully
drawn and wielded again by Thothmes III (*imperabat* 1479–
1447 B.C.) as soon as Death had removed Hatshepsut's restrain-

ing hand. The *karma* of the Militarism which governed the policy of 'the New Empire' for the next hundred years (*circa* 1479–1376 B.C.) could not be extinguished by Ikhnaton's passionate repudiation of a policy which he had inherited from four predecessors—any more than the nemesis of Nebuchadnezzar's militarism could be averted by Nabonidus' childish device of ignoring the unwelcome realities of his imperial heritage and seeking to forget the cares of state in the delights of archaeology.

In the history of the Ottoman Power Mehmed the Conqueror (*imperabat* A.D. 1451–81) deliberately limited his ambitions to the enterprise of making his *Pax Ottomanica* coterminous with the historic domain of Orthodox Christendom (not including its offshoot in Russia); and he resisted all temptations to encroach upon the adjoining domains of Western Christendom and the Iranic World. But—partly, no doubt, because his hand was forced by the aggressiveness of Ismā'īl Shāh Safawī—Mehmed's successor Selīm the Grim (*imperabat* A.D. 1512–20) broke Mehmed's self-denying ordinance in Asia, while Selīm's successor Suleymān (*imperabat* A.D. 1520–66) committed the further error—which was ultimately still more disastrous and which could not be excused on Selīm's plea of *force majeure*—of breaking the same self-denying ordinance in Europe as well. In consequence the Ottoman Power was rapidly worn down by the grinding friction of a perpetual warfare on two fronts against adversaries whom the 'Osmanlī could repeatedly defeat in the field but could never put out of action. And this Selimian and Suleymanian perversity came to be so deeply ingrained in the statecraft of the Sublime Porte that even the collapse that followed Suleymān's death did not produce any lasting revulsion in favour of a Mehmedian moderation. The squandered strength of the Ottoman Empire had no sooner been recruited by the statesmanship of the Köprülüs than it was expended by Qāra Mustafā on a new war of aggression against the Franks which was intended to carry the Ottoman frontier up to the eastern bank of the Rhine. Though he never came within sight of this objective, Qāra Mustafā did emulate Suleymān the Magnificent's feat of laying siege to Vienna. But in A.D. 1682–3, as in A.D. 1529, the boss of the Danubian carapace of Western Christendom proved to be too hard a nut for Ottoman arms to crack; and on this second occasion the 'Osmanlis did not fail before Vienna with impunity. The second Ottoman siege of Vienna evoked a Western counter-attack which continued, with no serious check, from A.D. 1683 to A.D. 1922, and which did not expend itself until the 'Osmanlis had not only been bereft of their empire but had even been compelled to renounce their ancestral Iranic culture as well, as the price of retaining possession of their homelands in Anatolia.

In thus wantonly stirring up a hornets' nest in Western Christendom, Qāra Mustafā, like Suleymān before him, was committing the classic error of Xerxes when the successor of Darius launched his war of aggression against Continental European Greece and thereby provoked a Hellenic counter-attack which immediately tore away from the Achaemenian Empire the Greek fringe of its dominions in Asia, and which ultimately led to the destruction of the Empire itself when the work begun by the sea-power of Athens under the auspices of Themistocles was taken up and completed by the land-power of Macedon under the auspices of Alexander.

It will be seen that, on the first of our two tests of ability to sheathe the sword, the rulers of universal states do not make a very good showing; and, if we now pass from the test of non-aggression against peoples beyond the pale to our second test of toleration towards the populations that are already living under the vaunted *Pax Oecumenica*, we shall find that Jovius fares hardly better in this second ordeal—though the receptivity which is characteristic of empire-builders might seem likely, on the face of it, to make toleration come easy to them.

The Roman Imperial Government, for example, made up its mind to tolerate Judaism and abode by this resolution in the face of severe and repeated Jewish provocations; but its forbearance was not equal to the more difficult moral feat of extending this toleration to a Jewish heresy that had set itself to convert the Hellenic World. In the very first collision between the Roman authorities and the Christian Church the Imperial Government took the extreme step of making the profession of Christianity a capital offence; and this declaration of war to the death was the only one of Nero's acts of savagery that was not rescinded by the tyrant's successors on the Imperial Throne. The motive of this proscription of Christianity as a *religio non licita* by the rulers of the Hellenic universal state is as significant as the sequel. The element in Christianity that was intolerable to the Imperial Government was the Christians' refusal to accept the Government's claim that it was entitled to compel its subjects to act against their consciences. The Christians were disputing the sword's prerogative; and, in defence of its *laesa majestas*, the weapon which Augustus had contrived to sheathe came shooting out of its scabbard again, like a snake out of its hole, to join battle, this time, with a spiritual power which could never be defeated by the strokes of a temporal weapon. So far from checking the propagation of Christianity, the martyrdoms proved to be the most effective agencies of conversion; and the eventual victory of the Christian martyr's spirit over the Roman ruler's blade bore out Tertullian's triumphantly defiant boast that Christian blood was seed.

The Achaemenian Government, like the Roman, set itself in principle to rule with the consent of the governed and was likewise only partially successful in living up to this policy in

practice. It did succeed in winning the allegiance of the Phoenicians and the Jews, but it failed in the long run to conciliate
either the Babylonians or the Egyptians. The magnanimity
with which the Tyrians were forgiven by Cambyses for their
refusal to serve against their Carthaginian kinsfolk, and the
Jews forgiven by Darius for Zerubbabel's abortive essay in
high treason, sufficed to confirm a loyalty which these two
Syriac peoples were inclined in any case to feel towards a
Great King whose sword had saved them from Babylonian op-
pressors in the one case and in the other from Greek competitors. But the conciliation of the Babylonian priesthood by
Cyrus and of the Egyptian priesthood by Darius was an
ephemeral *tour de force;* no tact or cajolery could permanently
reconcile the heirs of the Babylonic and Egyptiac Civilizations
to an alien domination; and Egypt and Babylon never ceased
to rise in revolt till Babylon was crushed by Xerxes and Egypt
by Ochus.

The 'Osmanlis had no better success in conciliating their
ra'īyeh—notwithstanding the wideness of the scope of the cultural, and even civil, autonomy that they conceded to them in
the *millet* system. The liberality of the system *de jure* was
marred by the high-handedness with which it was applied *de
facto;* the Ottoman Government was never able completely to
win the *ra'īyeh*'s hearts; and the perilously practical fashion in
which they displayed their disloyalty, as soon as a series of
Ottoman reverses afforded an opening for treachery on the
ra'īyeh's part, gave the successors of Selīm the Grim some reason to regret that this ruthless man of action had been deterred
(if the tale were true), by the joint exertions of his Grand Vezīr
Pīrī Pasha and his Sheykh-al-Islām Jemālī, from carrying out a
plan to exterminate the Orthodox Christian majority of his
subjects—as he did in fact exterminate an Imāmī Shī'ī minority.

In exerting himself, with success, to defeat Sultan Selīm's atrocious project, Sheykh Jemālī was moved not merely by his own personal feelings of humanity but by the standing orders of the Islamic Canon Law which it was the Sheykh's professional duty to uphold. The *Sherī'ah* required the Commander of the Faithful, or his deputy, to give quarter to non-Muslims who were 'People of the Book' if these forbore to resist the sword of Islam by force of arms, and so long as they gave and kept an undertaking to obey the Muslim authorities and to pay a super-tax. This was, in truth, the principle which had been followed by the Primitive Arab Muslim empire-builders, and their faith-fulness to it is one of the considerations that account for the amazing rapidity with which they accomplished their work. As soon as the preliminary raids gave place to permanent conquests on the grand scale, the Caliph 'Umar intervened to protect the conquered populations against the rapine, and even against the rights, of the Arab Muslim soldiery; it was 'Uthmān's unwill-ingness to abandon 'Umar's policy that cost the third of the Caliphs his life; and in this matter the Umayyads showed them-selves worthy successors of the 'Rightly Guided' Four. Mu-'āwiyah set an example of tolerance which was followed not only by the later Umayyads but also by the earlier 'Abbasids. Yet the latter days of the 'Abbasid régime did not pass without being disgraced by outbreaks of mob violence against Chris-tian subjects of the Caliphate who had by this time dwindled in numbers from a majority to a minority of the population as a result of the mass-conversions to Islam that heralded the break-up of the universal state and the approach of a social interregnum.

Our survey has revealed the suicidal importunity of a sword that has been sheathed after having once tasted blood. The pol-luted weapon will not rust in its scabbard, but must ever be itching to leap out again—as though the disembodied spirit of the would-be saviour who first had recourse to this sinister in-

strument could now find no rest until his sin of seeking salvation along a path of crime had been atoned for by the agency of
the very weapon which he once so perversely used. An instrument that is powerless to save may yet be potent to punish; the
penitently sheathed sword will still thirst implacably to carry
out this congenial duty; and it will have its way in the end when
it has Time for its ally. In the fulness of Time the din of battle
which has ebbed away towards the fringes of Civilization till it
has passed almost out of ear-shot will come welling back again
in the van of barbarian war-bands that have gained the upper
hand over the garrisons of the *limes* by learning from them, in
the effective school of a perpetual border warfare, the winning
tricks of the professional soldier's trade; or, more terrifying
still, the dreadful sound will come welling up again in the re-
surgence of an Internal Proletariat that has turned militant once
more—to the consternation of a Dominant Minority which has
been flattering itself that this *profanum vulgus* has long since
been cowed or cajoled into a settled habit of submissiveness.
The spectres of war and revolution that have latterly passed
into legend now once again stalk abroad, as of old, in the light
of day; and a *bourgeoisie* which has never before seen bloodshed now hastily throws up ring-walls round its open towns out
of any materials that come to hand: mutilated statues and dese-
crated altars and scattered drums of fallen columns and inscribed
blocks of marble reft from derelict public monuments. These
pacific inscriptions are now anachronisms; for the 'Indian Summer' is over; the 'Time of Troubles' has returned; and this
shocking calamity has descended upon a generation which has
been brought up in the illusory conviction that the bad times of
yore have gone for good!